FIFTH EDITION

Oracle PL/SQL Language

Pocket Reference

Steven Feuerstein, Bill Pribyl, and Chip Dawes

Beijing · Boston · Farnham · Sebastopol · Tokyo

Oracle PL/SQL Language Pocket Reference

by Steven Feuerstein, Bill Pribyl, and Chip Dawes

Printed in the United States of America.

Published by O'Reilly Media, Inc., 1005 Gravenstein Highway North, Sebastopol, CA 95472.

O'Reilly books may be purchased for educational, business, or sales promotional use. Online editions are also available for most titles (*http://safaribooksonline.com*). For more information, contact our corporate/institutional sales department: 800-998-9938 or *corporate@oreilly.com*.

Editor: Tim McGovern
Production Editor: Shiny Kalapurakkel
Copyeditor: Amanda Kersey
Proofreader: Kim Cofer
Indexer: Lucie Haskins
Interior Designer: David Futato
Cover Designer: Karen Montgomery
Illustrator: Rebecca Demarest

September 2015:   Fifth Edition

Revision History for the Fifth Edition

2015-09-04:   First Release

See *http://oreilly.com/catalog/errata.csp?isbn=9781491920008* for release details.

978-1-491-92000-8

[LSI]

Table of Contents

Oracle PL/SQL Language Pocket Reference

Introduction

The *Oracle PL/SQL Language Pocket Reference* is a quick reference guide to the PL/SQL programming language, which provides procedural extensions to the SQL relational database language.

The purpose of this pocket reference is to help PL/SQL users find the syntax of specific language elements. It is not a self-contained user guide; basic knowledge of the PL/SQL programming language is assumed. For more information, see the following O'Reilly books:

- *Oracle PL/SQL Programming*, Sixth Edition, by Steven Feuerstein with Bill Pribyl
- *Oracle PL/SQL Best Practices*, Second Edition, by Steven Feuerstein
- *Oracle Essentials*, Fifth Edition, by Rick Greenwald, Robert Stackowiak, and Jonathan Stern

Wherever a package, program, or function is supported only for a particular version of the Oracle database (e.g., Oracle Database 12c), we indicate this in the text.

Acknowledgments

We are grateful to all those who helped in the preparation of this book. In particular, thanks to Patrick Barel, Indu Janardanan, and Prachi Sharma for their technical reviews (though all mistakes and omissions remain the responsibility of the authors). Bryn Llewellyn gave us thorough and thoroughly helpful feedback on previous editions. Thanks as well to first-edition reviewers Eric J. Givler and Stephen Nelson and to second- and third-edition reviewer Jonathan Gennick. In addition, we appreciate all the good work by the O'Reilly crew, especially editor Tim McGovern, in editing and producing this book.

Conventions

UPPERCASE indicates PL/SQL keywords, as well as certain identifiers used by Oracle Corporation as built-in function and package names.

Italic indicates filenames and directories, as well as the first use of a term.

`Constant width` is used for code examples, literals, and identifiers.

`Constant width bold` indicates user input in examples showing an interaction.

[ ] enclose optional items in syntax descriptions.

{ } enclose a list of items in syntax descriptions; you must choose one item from the list.

| separates bracketed list items in syntax descriptions.

PL/SQL Language Fundamentals

This section summarizes the fundamental components of the PL/SQL language: characters, identifiers, literals, delimiters, use of comments and pragmas, and construction of statements and blocks.

PL/SQL Character Set

The PL/SQL language is constructed from letters, digits, symbols, and whitespace, as defined in the following table:

Type	Characters
Letters	A–Z, a–z
Digits	0—9
Symbols	~!@#$%*( )_-+=|:;"'< >,^.?/
Whitespace	Space, tab, newline, carriage return

Characters are grouped together into four lexical units: identifiers, literals, delimiters, and comments.

Identifiers

Identifiers are names for PL/SQL objects, such as constants, variables, exceptions, procedures, cursors, and reserved words. Identifiers have the following characteristics:

- Can be up to 30 characters in length
- Cannot include whitespace (space, tab, carriage return)
- Must start with a letter
- Can include a dollar sign ($), an underscore (_), and a pound sign (#)
- Are not case-sensitive

Using PL/SQL's reserved words as identifiers in your programs is not a good idea and can result in compilation or runtime errors that are difficult to troubleshoot.

If you enclose an identifier within double quotes, all but the first of these rules are ignored. For example, the following declaration is valid (although not exactly sensible):

```
DECLARE
    "1 ^abc"  VARCHAR2(100);
BEGIN
    IF "1 ^abc" IS NULL THEN ...
END;
```

Boolean, Numeric, and String Literals

Literals are specific values not represented by identifiers. For example, TRUE, 3.14159, 6.63E-34, 'Moby Dick', and NULL are all literals of type Boolean, number, or string. There are no complex datatype literals because their values are internal representations; complex types receive values through direct assignment or via constructors. Unlike the rest of PL/SQL, literals are case-sensitive. To embed single quotes within a string literal, place two single quotes next to each other.

You can define your own quoting mechanism for string literals in both your SQL and PL/SQL statements. Use the characters q' (q followed by a straight single quote) to designate the programmer-defined delimiter for your string literal. Terminate the literal string with the programmer-defined delimiter followed by a trailing single quote—for example, q'!my string!'. NCHAR and NVARCHAR delimiters are preceded by the letters nq, as in nq'^nchar string^'. This technique can simplify your code when consecutive single quotes appear within a string, such as the literals in a SQL statement. If you define your delimiter with one of the four bracketing characters ([{<, you must use the righthand version of the bracketing character as the closing delimiter. For example, q'[must be closed with]'.

See the following table for examples:

Literal	Actual value
'That''s Entertainment!'	That's Entertainment!
q'#That's Entertainment!#'	That's Entertainment!
'"The Raven"'	"The Raven"
'TZ=''CDT6CST'''	TZ='CDT6CST'
q'$TZ='CDT6CST'$'	TZ='CDT6CST'
q'[TZ='CDT6CST']'	TZ='CDT6CST'
''''	'
'''hello world'''	'hello world'
q'!'hello world'!'	'hello world'
''''''	''
q'['']'	''
nq'<Price='£'>'	Price='£'
nq'-WHERE name LIKE 'ñ'-'	WHERE name LIKE 'ñ'

Numeric Literals

Oracle may improve runtime performance if you make explicit the datatype of numeric literals. You can do so by including or excluding a decimal point or by using a trailing f or d, as shown in the following table:

Literal	Datatype
3.14159	NUMBER
42	INTEGER
0.0	NUMBER
3.14159f	BINARY_FLOAT
3.14159d	BINARY_DOUBLE

You can also use the named constants:

```
BINARY_FLOAT_NAN (not a number)
BINARY_FLOAT_INFINITY
BINARY_FLOAT_MAX_NORMAL
BINARY_FLOAT_MIN_NORMAL
BINARY_FLOAT_MAX_SUBNORMAL
BINARY_FLOAT_MIN_SUBNORMAL
```

as well as the BINARY_DOUBLE versions of these constants.

Datetime Interval Literals

The datetime interval datatypes represent a chronological interval expressed in terms of either years and months or days, hours, minutes, seconds, and fractional seconds. Literals of these datatypes require the keyword INTERVAL followed by the literal and format string(s). The interval must go from a larger field to a smaller one, so YEAR TO MONTH is valid, but MONTH TO YEAR is not. See the following table for examples:

Literal	Actual value
INTERVAL '1-3' YEAR TO MONTH	1 year and 3 months later
INTERVAL '125-11' YEAR(3) TO MONTH	125 years and 11 months later
INTERVAL '-18' MONTH	18 months earlier
INTERVAL '-48' HOUR	48 hours earlier

Literal	Actual value
INTERVAL '7 23:15' DAY TO MINUTE	7 days, 23 hours, 15 minutes later
INTERVAL '1 12:30:10.2' DAY TO SECOND	1 day, 12 hours, 30 minutes, 10.2 seconds later
INTERVAL '12:30:10.2' HOUR TO SECOND	12 hours, 30 minutes, 10.2 seconds later

Delimiters

Delimiters are symbols with special meaning, such as := (assignment operator), || (concatenation operator), and ; (statement delimiter). The following table lists the PL/SQL delimiters:

Delimiter	Description
;	Terminator (for statements and declarations)
+	Addition operator
–	Subtraction operator
*	Multiplication operator
/	Division operator
**	Exponentiation operator
||	Concatenation operator
:=	Assignment operator
=	Equality operator
<> and !=	Inequality operators
^= and ~=	Inequality operators
<	Less-than operator
<=	Less-than-or-equal-tooperator
>	Greater-than operator

Delimiter	Description
>=	Greater-than-or-equal-to operator
(and)	Expression or list delimiters
<< and >>	Label delimiters
,	Item separator
'	Literal delimiter
q' and '	Programmer-defined string literal delimiter
nq' and '	Programmer-defined NCHAR string literal delimiter
"	Quoted literal delimiter
:	Host variable indicator
%	Attribute indicator
.	Component indicator (as in *record.field* or *package.element*)
@	Remote database indicator (database link)
=>	Association operator (named notation)
..	Range operator (used in the FOR loop)
--	Single-line comment indicator
/* and */	Multiline comment delimiters

Comments

Comments are sections of code that exist to aid readability. The compiler ignores them.

A single-line comment begins with a double hyphen (--) and terminates at the end-of-line (newline). The compiler ignores all characters between the -- and the newline.

A multiline comment begins with slash asterisk (/*) and ends with asterisk slash (*/). The /* */ comment delimiters also can be used for a single-line comment. The following block demonstrates both kinds of comments:

```
DECLARE
    -- Two dashes comment out remainder of line.
    /* Everything is a comment until the compiler
       encounters the following symbol */
```

You cannot embed multiline comments within a multiline comment, so be careful during development if you comment out portions of code that include comments. The following code demonstrates this issue:

```
DECLARE
    /* Everything is a comment until the compiler
       /* This comment inside another WON'T work!*/
       encounters the following symbol. */

    /* Everything is a comment until the compiler
       -- This comment inside another WILL work!
       encounters the following symbol. */
```

Pragmas

The PRAGMA keyword is used to give instructions to the compiler. There are six types of pragmas in PL/SQL:

AUTONOMOUS_TRANSACTION

> Tells the compiler that the function, procedure, top-level anonymous PL/SQL block, object method, or database trigger executes in its own transaction space. See "Database Interaction" on page 35 for more information on this pragma.

EXCEPTION_INIT

> Tells the compiler to associate the specified error number with an identifier that has been declared an EXCEPTION in your current program or an accessible package. See "Exception Handling" on page 54 for more information on this pragma.

INLINE

> Tells the compiler whether calls to a subprogram should be replaced with a copy of the subprogram. See "Optimiz-

ing Compiler" on page 161 for more information on inline optimization.

RESTRICT_REFERENCES
> This pragma is deprecated; use DETERMINISTIC and PARALLEL_ENABLE instead.

SERIALLY_REUSABLE
> Tells the runtime engine that package data should not persist between references. This is used to reduce per-user memory requirements when the package data is needed only for the duration of the call and not for the duration of the session. See "Packages" on page 129 for more information on this pragma.

UDF (Oracle Database 12c and higher)
> Tells the compiler that you intend for your user-defined function to be invoked primarily from SQL rather than PL/SQL. This allows Oracle to optimize for performance inside SQL (at the possible expense of its performance in PL/SQL).

Statements

A PL/SQL program is composed of one or more logical statements. A *statement* is terminated by a semicolon delimiter. The physical end-of-line marker in a PL/SQL program is ignored by the compiler, except to terminate a single-line comment (initiated by the -- symbol).

Block Structure

Each PL/SQL program is a *block* consisting of a standard set of elements, identified by keywords (see Figure 1). The block determines the scope of declared elements and how exceptions are handled and propagated. A block can be *anonymous* or *named*. Named blocks include functions, procedures, packages, and triggers.

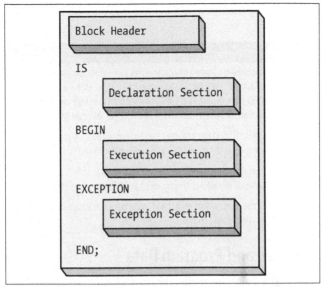

Figure 1. The PL/SQL block structure

Here is an example of an anonymous block:

```
DECLARE
    today DATE DEFAULT SYSDATE;
BEGIN
    -- Display the date.
    DBMS_OUTPUT.PUT_LINE ('Today is ' || today);
END;
```

Here is a named block that performs the same action:

```
CREATE OR REPLACE PROCEDURE show_the_date
IS
    today DATE DEFAULT SYSDATE;
BEGIN
    -- Display the date.
    DBMS_OUTPUT.PUT_LINE ('Today is ' || today);
END show_the_date;
```

The following table summarizes the sections of a PL/SQL block:

Section	Description
Header	Required for named blocks. Specifies the way the program is called by other PL/SQL blocks. Anonymous blocks do not have a header. They start with the DECLARE keyword if there is a declaration section, or with the BEGIN keyword if there are no declarations.
Declaration	Optional; declares variables, cursors, types, and local programs that are used in the block's execution and exception sections.
Execution	Contains statements that are executed when the block is run; optional in package specifications and type specifications.
Exception	Optional; describes error-handling behavior for exceptions raised in the executable section.

Variables and Program Data

PL/SQL programs normally are used to manipulate database information. You commonly do this by declaring variables and data structures in your programs, and then working with that PL/SQL-specific data.

A *variable* is a named instantiation of a data structure declared in a PL/SQL block (either locally or in a package). Unless you declare a variable as a CONSTANT, its value can be changed at any time in your program.

The following table summarizes the different types of program data:

Type	Description
Scalar	Variables made up of a single value, such as a number, date, or Boolean.
Composite	Variables made up of multiple values, such as a record, collection, or instance of a user-defined object type. See the sections "Records in PL/SQL" on page 62, "Collections in PL/SQL" on page 66, and "Object-Oriented Features" on page 137.

Type	Description
Reference	Logical pointers to values or cursors.
LOB	Variables containing large object (LOB) locators.

Scalar Datatypes

Scalar datatypes divide into four families: number, character, datetime, and Boolean. Subtypes further define a base datatype by restricting the values or size of the base datatype.

Numeric datatypes

Numeric datatypes represent real numbers, integers, and floating-point numbers. They are stored as NUMBER, PLS_INTEGER, and IEEE floating-point storage types.

Decimal numeric datatypes store fixed and floating-point numbers of just about any size. They include the subtypes NUMBER, DEC, DECIMAL, NUMERIC, FLOAT, REAL, and DOUBLE PRECISION. The maximum precision of a variable with type NUMBER is 38 digits, which yields a range of values from `1.0E-129` through `9.999E125`.

Variables of type NUMBER can be declared with precision and scale, as follows:

```
NUMBER(precision, scale)
```

where *precision* is the number of digits, and *scale* is the number of digits to the right (positive scale) or left (negative scale) of the decimal point at which rounding occurs. Legal values for *scale* range from −84 to 127. The following table shows examples of precision and scale:

Declaration	Assigned value	Stored value
NUMBER	6.02	6.02
NUMBER(4)	8675	8675
NUMBER(4)	8675309	Error

Declaration	Assigned value	Stored value
NUMBER(12,5)	3.14159265	3.14159
NUMBER(12,−5)	8675309	8700000

Oracle provides a variety of datatypes to store whole numbers: BINARY_INTEGER, INTEGER, INT, SMALLINT, NATURAL, NATURALN, POSITIVE, POSITIVEN, SIGNTYPE, and PLS_INTEGER.

Binary integer datatypes store signed integers in the range of $-2^{31} + 1$ to $2^{31} - 1$. The subtypes include NATURAL (0 through $2^{31} - 1$) and POSITIVE (1 through $2^{31} - 1$) together with the NOT NULL variations NATURALN and POSITIVEN. SIGN-TYPE is restricted to three values (−1, 0, 1). PLS_INTEGER is an unconstrained subtype (alias) of BINARY_INTEGER.

SIMPLE_INTEGER has the same range as BINARY_INTEGER except that it does not allow for null values and does not raise an exception if an overflow occurs. For example, 2147483647 + 1 = −2147483648 (note the negative value!). SIMPLE_INTE-GER datatypes can result in significantly faster execution speeds when the PL/SQL code is compiled to native machine code.

IEEE 754–compliant floating-point numbers are available in both SQL and PL/SQL. These subtypes are the single-precision BINARY_FLOAT and the double-precision BINARY_DOU-BLE. Because these datatypes require less memory and use native machine arithmetic, they perform much better for scientific or engineering applications that are computer-intensive or that require comparison to infinity or not a number (NaN). These two datatypes have binary precision instead of the decimal precision in the NUMBER family. So, if you are developing financial applications that are concerned with rounding errors or require decimal precision, you probably should not use these floating-point datatypes.

The following table lists the PL/SQL numeric datatypes with ANSI and IBM compatibility. In this table:

- *precision* is the precision for the subtype.
- *scale* is the scale of the subtype.
- *binary* is the binary precision of the subtype.

PL/SQL datatype	Compatibility	Oracle database datatype
DEC(*precision,scale*)	ANSI	NUMBER(*precision,scale*)
DECIMAL(*precision,scale*)	IBM	NUMBER(*precision,scale*)
DOUBLE PRECISION	ANSI	NUMBER
FLOAT(*binary*)	ANSI, IBM	NUMBER
INT	ANSI	NUMBER(38)
INTEGER	ANSI, IBM	NUMBER(38)
NUMERIC(*precision,scale*)	ANSI	NUMBER(*precision,scale*)
REAL	ANSI	NUMBER
SMALLINT	ANSI, IBM	NUMBER(38)
BINARY_FLOAT	IEEE 754	BINARY_FLOAT
BINARY_ DOUBLE	IEEE 754	BINARY_ DOUBLE

Character datatypes

Character datatypes store alphanumeric text and are manipulated by character functions. As with the numeric family, there are several subtypes in the character family, shown in the following table:

Family	Description
CHAR	Fixed-length alphanumeric strings. Valid sizes are 1 to 32,767 bytes.
VARCHAR2	Variable-length alphanumeric strings. Valid sizes are 1 to 32,767 bytes.

Family	Description
LONG	Variable-length alphanumeric strings. Valid sizes are 1 to 32,760 bytes. LONG is included primarily for backward compatibility; instead use VARCHAR2(32767), CLOB, BLOB, or NCLOB for large character strings.
RAW	Variable-length binary strings. Valid sizes are 1 to 32,767 bytes (which is larger than the database limit of 2,000). RAW data does not undergo character set conversion when selected from a remote database.
LONG RAW	Variable-length binary strings. Valid sizes are 1 to 32,760 bytes. LONG RAW is included primarily for backward compatibility; BLOB and BFILE are the preferred datatypes for large binary data.
ROWID	Fixed-length binary data. Every row in a database has a physical address or ROWID. A ROWID has four parts in base 64: *OOOOOOFFFBBBBBBRRR* where: • *OOOOOO* is the object number. • *FFFF* is the absolute or relative file number. • *BBBBBB* is the block number within the file. • *RRR* is the row number within the block.
UROWID	Universal ROWID. Variable-length hexadecimal string depicting a logical, physical, or non-Oracle row identifier. Valid sizes are up to 4,000 bytes.

Unicode character datatypes

The standard WE8MSWIN1252 or WE8ISO8859P2 character set does not support some languages, such as Chinese and Greek. To support multiple languages, the database allows two character sets—the *database character set* and a *Unicode character set*, sometimes called the *national character set* (NLS).

The two NLS datatypes, NCHAR and NVARCHAR2, are used to represent data in the Unicode character set. NCHAR values are fixed-length character data; the maximum length is 32,767 bytes. NVARCHAR2 values are variable-length character data; the maximum length also is 32,767 bytes.

Datetime datatypes

The datetime datatypes are DATE, TIMESTAMP, TIMESTAMP WITH TIME ZONE, and TIMESTAMP WITH LOCAL TIME ZONE. There are also two interval datatypes, INTERVAL YEAR TO MONTH and INTERVAL DAY TO SECOND.

DATE values are fixed-length, date-plus-time values. The DATE datatype can store dates from January 1, 4712 BC to December 31, 9999 AD. Each DATE includes the century, year, month, day, hour, minute, and second. Subsecond granularity is not supported via the DATE datatype; use one of the TIME-STAMP datatypes instead. The time portion of a DATE defaults to midnight (12:00:00 a.m.) if it is not included explicitly.

TIMESTAMP values store date and time to subsecond granularity. The subsecond precision (the number of digits to the right of the decimal) either defaults to 6 or is set to 0 through 9 digits by declaration, as in:

```
DECLARE
   mytime_declared    TIMESTAMP(9); -- max precision
   mytime_default     TIMESTAMP;    -- default 6
digits precision
   mytime_to_seconds TIMESTAMP(0); -- no fractional
seconds
```

TIMESTAMP WITH TIME ZONE values store date and time values like a TIMESTAMP but also store the hourly offset from Coordinated Universal Time (UTC, which is essentially equivalent to Greenwich Mean Time). As with TIMESTAMP, the subsecond precision is 0 to 9 digits, either declared or inherited from the default 6 digits of precision:

```
DECLARE
   mytime_declared TIMESTAMP(9) WITH TIME ZONE;
   mytime_default  TIMESTAMP WITH TIME ZONE;
```

TIMESTAMP WITH LOCAL TIME ZONE values store date and time values together with the UTC offset, like a TIME-STAMP WITH TIME ZONE. The principal difference between these timestamp datatypes occurs when values are saved to or retrieved from a database table. TIMESTAMP WITH LOCAL TIME ZONE values are converted to the database time zone and saved without an offset. The values retrieved from the database table are converted from the database time zone to the session's time zone.

The offset from UTC for both TIMESTAMP WITH TIME ZONE and TIMESTAMP WITH LOCAL TIME ZONE can be hours and minutes or a time zone region (found in the V$TIMEZONE_NAMES data dictionary view) with the optional daylight savings time name (also found in V$TIME-ZONE_NAMES). For example:

```
ALTER SESSION SET NLS_TIMESTAMP_TZ_FORMAT=
    'DD-Mon-YYYY HH24:MI:SS.FF TZR';

DECLARE
    my_tswtz    TIMESTAMP(4) WITH TIME ZONE;
BEGIN
    my_tswtz := '31-MAR-2016 07:32:45.1234 US/
Pacific';
```

INTERVAL YEAR TO MONTH values store a period of time in years and months:

```
DECLARE
    myy2m INTERVAL YEAR TO MONTH;
BEGIN
    myy2m := INTERVAL '1-6' YEAR TO MONTH; --
interval of 18 months
```

INTERVAL DAY TO SECOND values store a period of time in days, hours, minutes, seconds, and fractional seconds:

```
DECLARE
    myd2s INTERVAL DAY TO SECOND;
BEGIN
    myd2s := INTERVAL '2 10:32:15.678' DAY TO SECOND;
```

BOOLEAN datatype

The BOOLEAN datatype can store one of *three* values: TRUE, FALSE, or NULL. BOOLEAN variables usually are used in logical control structures such as IF . . . THEN or LOOP statements.

The following truth tables show the results of logical AND, OR, and NOT operations with PL/SQL's three-value Boolean model:

AND	TRUE	FALSE	NULL
TRUE	TRUE	FALSE	NULL
FALSE	FALSE	FALSE	FALSE
NULL	NULL	FALSE	NULL

OR	TRUE	FALSE	NULL
TRUE	TRUE	TRUE	TRUE
FALSE	TRUE	FALSE	NULL
NULL	TRUE	NULL	NULL

NOT (TRUE)	NOT (FALSE)	NOT (NULL)
FALSE	TRUE	NULL

LOB Datatypes

PL/SQL supports a number of large object (LOB) datatypes, which can store objects up to 8 terabytes in size, or even up to 128 TB, depending on database block size. Unlike the scalar datatypes, variables declared for LOBs use *locators*, or pointers to the actual data. LOBs are manipulated in PL/SQL using the built-in package DBMS_LOB. The LOB datatypes are:

BFILE

  File locators pointing to read-only large binary objects in operating system files. With BFILEs, the large objects are outside the database, and the maximum size is system-dependent.

BLOB
> LOB locators that point to large binary objects inside the
> database.

CLOB
> LOB locators that point to large character (alphanumeric)
> objects inside the database.

NCLOB
> LOB locators that point to large Unicode character objects
> inside the database.

Implicit Datatype Conversions

Whenever PL/SQL detects that a datatype conversion is necessary, it attempts to change the values as required to perform the
operation. Not all values in each datatype can be converted to
another datatype. For example, an attempt to convert
BINARY_FLOAT_NAN to a number datatype will raise an
INVALID NUMBER exception.

NULLs in PL/SQL

PL/SQL represents unknown or inapplicable values as NULL
values. Because a NULL is unknown, a NULL is never equal or
not equal to anything (including another NULL value). In
addition, most functions and operators return a NULL when
passed a NULL argument. You cannot check for equality or
inequality to NULL; therefore, you must use the IS NULL or IS
NOT NULL syntax to check for NULL values.

Here is an example of the IS NULL syntax used to check the
value of a variable:

```
BEGIN
   /* Correct usage */
   IF myvar IS NULL THEN ...

   /* Dangerous! Always evaluates to NULL */
   IF myvar = NULL THEN ...
```

There are several ways in SQL and PL/SQL to substitute a non-null value for a null variable or expression. NVL is commonly used:

```
NVL (exprn1, exprn2)
```

With NVL, Oracle will always evaluate both arguments, even if *exprn1* is not null. A potentially more efficient function is COALESCE:

```
COALESCE(exprn1, exprn2 [, exprn3, ...] )
```

COALESCE has two distinct characteristics: first, it accepts more than two arguments; second, it uses short-circuit evaluation, meaning it stops looking for a non-null value when it finds one (and, therefore, does not evaluate every expression in the list, which NVL does).

Declaring Variables

Before you can use a variable, you must first declare it in the declaration section of your PL/SQL block or in a package as a global. When you declare a variable, PL/SQL allocates memory for the variable's value and names the storage location so that the value can be retrieved and changed. The syntax for a variable declaration is:

```
variable_name [CONSTANT] datatype [NOT NULL]
   [{ := | DEFAULT } initial_value];
```

Constrained declarations

A programmer may constrain certain datatypes at declaration so that variables have a size, scale, or precision that is less than the maximum allowed. Some examples:

```
total_sales     NUMBER(15,2);   -- Constrained
emp_id          VARCHAR2(9);    -- Constrained
company_number  NUMBER;         -- Unconstrained
book_title      VARCHAR2;       -- Not valid
```

Constrained declarations can require less memory than unconstrained declarations. Not all datatypes can be declared unconstrained; VARCHAR2 is a notable exception.

Constants

The CONSTANT keyword in a declaration requires an initial value and does not allow that value to be changed in the program. For example:

```
min_order_qty    NUMBER(1) CONSTANT := 5;
```

Default values

The PL/SQL runtime engine assigns a default value of NULL to each variable you explicitly declare.[1] If you want to initialize a variable to a value other than NULL, you can do so in the declaration with either the assignment operator (:=) or the DEFAULT keyword:

```
counter    BINARY_INTEGER := 0;
priority   VARCHAR2(8)    DEFAULT 'LOW';
```

A NOT NULL constraint can be appended to the variable's datatype declaration to indicate that NULL is not a valid value. If you add the NOT NULL constraint, you must explicitly assign an initial value for that variable.

Anchored Declarations

Use the %TYPE attribute to *anchor* the datatype of a scalar variable to either another variable or to a column in a database table or view. Use %ROWTYPE to anchor a record's declaration to a cursor or table (see "Records in PL/SQL" on page 62 for more details on the %ROWTYPE attribute).

---

1 There is one exception to this rule: associative arrays are *not* null when declared, and there is no way to make them null. However, when declared, associative arrays have no elements, a state unsurprisingly known as "empty."

The following block shows several variations of anchored declarations:

```
DECLARE
    tot_sales NUMBER(20,2);

    -- Anchor to a local variable
    monthly_sales tot_sales%TYPE;

    -- Anchor to a database column
    v_ename employee.last_name%TYPE;

    -- Anchor to a cursor
    CURSOR mycur IS SELECT * FROM employee;
    myrec mycur%ROWTYPE;
```

The NOT NULL clause on a variable declaration (but not on a database column definition) follows the %TYPE anchoring and requires anchored declarations to have a default in their declaration. The default value for an anchored declaration can be different from that for the base declaration:

```
tot_sales       NUMBER(20,2) NOT NULL DEFAULT 0;
monthly_sales   tot_sales%TYPE DEFAULT 10;
```

Programmer-Defined Subtypes

PL/SQL allows you to define unconstrained scalar subtypes, which you might want to do for greater "self-documentation" of your code or for future-proofing. An unconstrained subtype provides an alias to the original underlying datatype; for example:

```
CREATE OR REPLACE PACKAGE std_types
IS
    -- Declare reusable app-specific type
    SUBTYPE dollar_amt_t IS NUMBER;
END std_types;

CREATE OR REPLACE PROCEDURE process_money
IS
```

```
-- Use standardized type declared in package
credit std_types.dollar_amt_t;
```

A constrained subtype limits or constrains the new datatype to a subset of the original datatype. For example, POSITIVE is a constrained subtype of BINARY_INTEGER. The declaration for POSITIVE in the STANDARD package is:

```
SUBTYPE POSITIVE IS BINARY_INTEGER RANGE
1..2147483647;
```

You can define your own constrained subtypes in your programs:

```
PACKAGE std_types
IS
    SUBTYPE currency_t IS NUMBER (15, 2);
END;
```

Conditional and Sequential Control

PL/SQL includes conditional (IF, CASE) structures as well as sequential control (GOTO, NULL) constructs.

Conditional Control Statements

There are several varieties of IF-THEN-ELSE and CASE structures.

IF-THEN combination

```
IF condition THEN
    executable statement(s)
END IF;
```

For example:

```
IF caller_type = 'VIP' THEN
    generate_response('GOLD');
END IF;
```

IF-THEN-ELSE combination

```
IF condition THEN
   TRUE sequence_of_executable_statement(s)
ELSE
   FALSE (or NULL) sequence_of_statement(s)
END IF;
```

For example:

```
IF caller_type = 'VIP' THEN
   generate_response('GOLD');
ELSE
   generate_response('BRONZE');
END IF;
```

Note that a condition that evaluates to NULL at runtime will cause control to branch to the ELSE clause.

IF-THEN-ELSIF combination

Oracle's else-if condition allows testing a second conditional expression. Note that the second letter "e" is missing in the ELSIF keyword:

```
IF condition-1 THEN
   statements-1
ELSIF condition-N THEN
 statements-N
[ELSE
   ELSE statements]
END IF;
```

For example:

```
IF caller_type = 'VIP' THEN
   generate_response('GOLD');
ELSIF priority_client THEN
   generate_response('SILVER');
ELSE
   generate_response('BRONZE');
END IF;
```

CASE statement

There are two types of CASE statements: simple and searched.

A simple CASE statement is similar to an IF-THEN-ELSIF structure. The statement has a switch expression immediately after the keyword CASE. The expression is evaluated and compared to the value in each WHEN clause. The first WHEN clause with a matching value is executed, and then control passes to the next statement following the END CASE. For example:

```
CASE region_id
   WHEN 'NE' THEN
      mgr_name := 'MINER';
   WHEN 'SE' THEN
      mgr_name := 'KOOI';
   ELSE
      mgr_name := 'LANE';
END CASE;
```

If a switch expression evaluates to NULL, the ELSE case is the only one that can possibly match; WHEN NULL will never match because the database performs an equality comparison on the expressions.

Both the CASE statement and the CASE expression (see next section) should include an ELSE clause that will execute statements if no WHEN clause evaluates to TRUE, because PL/SQL's runtime engine will raise an exception if it finds no matching expression.

The searched CASE statement does not have a switch; instead, each WHEN clause has a complete Boolean expression. The first matching WHEN clause is executed, and control passes to the next statement following the END CASE; for example:

```
CASE
   WHEN region_id = 'EAME' THEN
      mgr_name := 'SCHMIDT';
   WHEN division = 'SALES' THEN
      mgr_name := 'KENNEDY';
```

```
      ELSE mgr_name := 'GUPTA';
   END CASE;
```

CASE expression

There are also two types of CASE expressions: simple and searched. You can use CASE expressions anywhere that expressions are valid in your SQL or PL/SQL programs.

A simple CASE expression lets you choose an expression to evaluate based on a scalar value that you provide as input. The following example shows a simple CASE expression being used with the built-in DBMS_OUTPUT package to output the value of a Boolean variable. DBMS_OUTPUT.PUT_LINE is not overloaded to handle Boolean types, so in this example, the CASE expression converts the Boolean value in a character string, which PUT_LINE can then handle:

```
DECLARE
   boolean_true BOOLEAN := TRUE;
   boolean_false BOOLEAN := FALSE;
   boolean_null BOOLEAN;

   FUNCTION b2vc (flag IN BOOLEAN)
      RETURN VARCHAR2 IS
   BEGIN
      RETURN
         CASE flag
            WHEN TRUE THEN 'True'
            WHEN FALSE THEN 'False'
            ELSE 'Null'
         END;
   END;

BEGIN
   DBMS_OUTPUT.PUT_LINE (b2vc(boolean_true));
   DBMS_OUTPUT.PUT_LINE (b2vc(boolean_false));
   DBMS_OUTPUT.PUT_LINE( b2vc(boolean_null));
END;
```

A searched CASE expression evaluates a list of expressions to find the first one that evaluates to TRUE, and then returns the results of an associated expression. In the following example, a searched CASE expression returns the proper bonus value for any given salary:

```
DECLARE
  salary NUMBER := 20000;
  employee_id NUMBER := 36325;

  PROCEDURE give_bonus
    (emp_id IN NUMBER, bonus_amt IN NUMBER) IS
  BEGIN
    DBMS_OUTPUT.PUT_LINE(emp_id);
    DBMS_OUTPUT.PUT_LINE(bonus_amt);
  END;

BEGIN
  give_bonus(employee_id,
    CASE
      WHEN salary >= 10000
          AND salary <=20000 THEN 1500
      WHEN salary > 20000
          AND salary <= 40000 THEN 1000
      WHEN salary > 40000 THEN 500
      ELSE 0
    END);
END;
```

Sequential Control Statements

PL/SQL provides a GOTO statement and a NULL statement to aid in sequential control operations.

GOTO

Although rarely used, the GOTO statement performs unconditional branching to a named label. At least one executable statement must follow the label (the NULL statement can be this necessary executable statement). The format of a GOTO statement is:

```
    GOTO label_name;
```

For example:

```
BEGIN
    GOTO second_output;

    DBMS_OUTPUT.PUT_LINE('Will never execute.');

    <<second_output>>
    DBMS_OUPUT.PUT_LINE('We are here!);
END
```

There are several scope restrictions on where a GOTO can branch control. A GOTO:

- Can branch out of an IF statement, LOOP, or subblock.

- Cannot branch into an IF statement, LOOP, or subblock.

- Cannot branch from one section of an IF statement to another (from the IF-THEN section to the ELSE section is illegal).

- Cannot branch into or out of a subprogram.

- Cannot branch from the exception section to the executable section of a PL/SQL block.

- Cannot branch from the executable section to the exception section of a PL/SQL block, although a RAISE does this.

NULL

The NULL statement is an executable statement that does nothing. It is useful when an executable statement must follow a GOTO label or to aid readability in an IF-THEN-ELSE structure. For example:

```
IF :report.selection = 'DETAIL' THEN
    exec_detail_report;
ELSE
```

```
        NULL;
    END IF;
```

Loops

The LOOP construct allows you to execute a sequence of statements repeatedly. There are three types of loops: simple (infinite), FOR, and WHILE.

You can use the EXIT statement to break out of the LOOP and pass control to the statement following the END LOOP. Use the CONTINUE statement, described later, to break out of the current loop iteration and pass control to the next loop iteration.

Simple Loop

```
LOOP
    executable_statement(s)
END LOOP;
```

The simple loop should contain an EXIT or EXIT WHEN unless you want it to execute infinitely. Use the simple loop when you want the body of the loop to execute at least once. For example:

```
LOOP
    FETCH company_cur INTO company_rec;
    EXIT WHEN company_cur%ROWCOUNT > 5 OR
        company_cur%NOTFOUND;
    process_company(company_cur);
END LOOP;
```

Numeric FOR Loop

```
FOR loop_index IN [REVERSE]
        lowest_number..highest_number
LOOP
    executable_statement(s)
END LOOP;
```

The PL/SQL runtime engine automatically declares the loop index a PLS_INTEGER variable, and you don't want or need to declare a variable with that name yourself. The *lowest_number* and *highest_number* ranges can be variables but are evaluated only once—on initial entry into the loop. The REVERSE keyword causes PL/SQL to start with the *highest_number* and decrement down to the *lowest_number*. For example, this code:

```
BEGIN
   FOR counter IN 1 .. 4
   LOOP
      DBMS_OUTPUT.PUT(counter);
   END LOOP;
   DBMS_OUTPUT.NEW_LINE;

   FOR counter IN REVERSE 1 .. 4
   LOOP
      DBMS_OUTPUT.PUT(counter);
   END LOOP;
   DBMS_OUTPUT.NEW_LINE;
END;
```

yields the following output:

```
1234
4321
```

Cursor FOR Loop

```
FOR loop_index IN
      {cursor_name | (SELECT statement)}
LOOP
   executable_statement(s)
END LOOP;
```

The PL/SQL runtime engine implicitly declares the loop index as a record of *cursor_name*%ROWTYPE; do not explicitly declare a variable with that name.

The cursor FOR loop automatically opens the cursor, fetches all rows identified by the cursor, and then closes the cursor. You can embed the SELECT statement directly in the cursor FOR loop or use a previously declared cursor; for example:

```
FOR emp_rec IN emp_cur
LOOP
    IF emp_rec.title = 'Oracle Programmer'
    THEN
        give_raise(emp_rec.emp_id,30)
    END IF;
END LOOP;
```

The cursor FOR loop is an elegant, *declarative* construct (you tell the database to fetch every row in the cursor without specifying *how* to do it). Internally, Oracle will attempt to optimize such a fetch loop by retrieving 100 rows at a time, but you may still want to explicitly use BULK COLLECT and FORALL. See "Bulk Binds" on page 79 for information on these statements.

WHILE Loop

```
WHILE condition
LOOP
    executable_statement(s)
END LOOP;
```

Use the WHILE loop in cases where you may not want the loop body to execute even once:

```
WHILE NOT end_of_analysis
LOOP
    perform_analysis;
    get_next_record;
    IF analysis_cursor%NOTFOUND
        AND next_step IS NULL
    THEN
        end_of_analysis := TRUE;
    END IF;
END LOOP;
```

"Repeat Until" Loop Emulation

PL/SQL does not directly support a REPEAT UNTIL construct, but a modified simple loop can emulate one. The syntax for this emulated REPEAT UNTIL loop is:

```
LOOP
    executable_statement(s)
    EXIT WHEN boolean_condition;
END LOOP;
```

Use such a loop when executing iterations indefinitely before conditionally terminating the loop.

EXIT Statement

```
EXIT [WHEN condition];
```

If you do not include a WHEN clause, EXIT will terminate the loop unconditionally. Otherwise, the loop terminates only if the Boolean *condition* evaluates to TRUE. The EXIT statement is optional and can appear anywhere in the loop.

CONTINUE Statement

The CONTINUE statement terminates the current iteration of a loop, passing control to the next iteration. The format of a CONTINUE statement is:

```
CONTINUE [label_name][WHEN boolean_expression];
```

The optional *label_name* identifies which loop to terminate. If no *label_name* is specified, the innermost loop's current iteration is terminated.

Like the EXIT statement, the CONTINUE statement is optional and can appear anywhere in the loop. The CONTINUE statement can be used to pass control out of a loop, optionally crossing loop boundaries, but cannot pass control out across a procedure, function, or method boundary.

The following example uses CONTINUE to branch out of an inner loop as well an outer loop:

```
DECLARE
  TYPE dow_tab_t IS TABLE OF VARCHAR2(10);
  dow_tab dow_tab_t := dow_tab_t('Sunday'
    ,'Monday','Tuesday','Wednesday','Thursday'
    ,'Friday','Saturday');
BEGIN
  <<day_loop>>
  FOR counter IN 2 .. 6 LOOP
    --Skip Wednesdays
    CONTINUE day_loop
      WHEN dow_tab(counter)='Wednesday';
    DBMS_OUTPUT.PUT_LINE (dow_tab(counter));
  END LOOP;
END;
```

This yields the following output:

```
Monday
Tuesday
Thursday
Friday
```

This example shows how control may be passed from within an inner loop to the next iteration of an outer loop:

```
BEGIN
  <<outer_loop>>
  FOR outer_counter IN 1 .. 3 LOOP
    DBMS_OUTPUT.PUT_LINE(outer_counter);
    <<inner_loop>>
    FOR inner_counter IN 10 .. 15 LOOP
      CONTINUE outer_loop
        WHEN outer_counter > 1
              AND inner_counter = 12;
      DBMS_OUTPUT.PUT_LINE('...'||inner_counter);
    END LOOP;
  END LOOP;
END;
```

This yields the following output:

```
1
...10
```

```
...11
...12
...13
...14
...15
2
...10
...11
3
...10
...11
```

Loop Labels

Loops can be optionally labeled to improve readability and execution control, as shown in the preceding code. The label must appear immediately in front of the statement that initiates the loop.

The following example demonstrates the use of loop labels to qualify variables within a loop and also to terminate nested and outer loops:

```
<<year_loop>>
FOR yearind IN 1 .. 20
LOOP
    <<month_loop>>
    LOOP
        ...
        IF year_loop.yearind > 10
        THEN
            EXIT year_loop;
        END IF;
    END LOOP month_loop;
END LOOP year_loop;
```

Database Interaction

PL/SQL is tightly integrated with the underlying SQL layer of the Oracle database. You can execute SQL statements (SELECT, INSERT, UPDATE, DELETE, MERGE, LOCK TABLE) directly in PL/SQL programs. You also can execute Data Definition Language (DDL) statements through the use of dynamic SQL. In addition, you can manage transactions with COMMIT, ROLLBACK, and other Data Control Language (DCL) statements.

Sequences in PL/SQL

Sequences are frequently used to generate keys in an Oracle database. In code that predates Oracle Database 11g, it was customary to select from DUAL to obtain a sequence's NEXTVAL or CURRVAL as follows:

```
/* No longer necessary! */
SELECT my_sequence.NEXTVAL
   INTO my_variable FROM dual;
```

However, NEXTVAL and CURRVAL are now available anywhere in your program in which a number expression can appear. For example:

```
my_variable := my_sequence.NEXTVAL;
```

Transaction Management

The Oracle database provides a transaction model based on a unit of work. A transaction begins with the first change to data and ends with either a COMMIT or a ROLLBACK. Transactions can span multiple PL/SQL blocks, or multiple transactions can be in a single PL/SQL block. The PL/SQL-supported transaction statements include COMMIT, ROLLBACK, SAVEPOINT, SET TRANSACTION, and LOCK TABLE, described in the following sections.

COMMIT

```
COMMIT [WORK] [comment_text];
```

COMMIT makes the database changes permanent and visible to other database sessions. The WORK keyword is optional and aids only readability; it is rarely used. The COMMENT text is optional and can be up to 50 characters in length. It is germane only to in-doubt distributed (two-phase commit) transactions. The database statement COMMIT FORCE, also relevant for distributed transactions, is not directly supported in PL/SQL, but can be invoked using the built-in procedure DBMS_TRANSACTION.COMMIT_FORCE.

ROLLBACK

```
ROLLBACK [WORK] [TO [SAVEPOINT] savepoint_name];
```

ROLLBACK undoes the changes made in the current transaction either to the beginning of the transaction or to a *savepoint*. A savepoint is a named processing point in a transaction, created with the SAVEPOINT statement. Rolling back to a savepoint is a partial rollback of a transaction, wiping out all changes (and savepoints) that occurred later than the named savepoint.

SAVEPOINT

```
SAVEPOINT savepoint_name;
```

SAVEPOINT establishes a savepoint in the current transaction. *savepoint_name* is an undeclared identifier. More than one savepoint can be established within a transaction. If you reuse a savepoint name, that savepoint is moved to the later position, and you will not be able to roll back to the initial savepoint position.

SET TRANSACTION

```
SET TRANSACTION READ ONLY;
SET TRANSACTION ISOLATION LEVEL SERIALIZABLE;
SET TRANSACTION USE ROLLBACK SEGMENT rbseg_name;
```

SET TRANSACTION has three transaction control functions:

READ ONLY

This marks the beginning of a read-only transaction. It indicates to the Oracle database that a read-consistent view of the database is to be enforced for the transaction (the default is for the statement). This read-consistent view means that only changes committed before the transaction begins are visible for the duration of the transaction. The transaction is ended with either a COMMIT or a ROLLBACK. Only LOCK TABLE, SELECT, SELECT INTO, OPEN, FETCH, CLOSE, COMMIT, and ROLLBACK statements are permitted during a read-only transaction. Issuing other statements, such as INSERT or UPDATE, in a read-only transaction results in an ORA-1456 error.

ISOLATION LEVEL SERIALIZABLE

Similar to a READ ONLY transaction in that transaction-level read consistency is enforced rather than the default statement-level read consistency. Serializable transactions do allow changes to data, however.

USE ROLLBACK SEGMENT

If your database is using rollback segments for undo management, as opposed to Oracle's recommended automatic undo management, this statement tells the database to use the specifically named rollback segment *rbseg_name*. For example, if we know that our large rollback segment is named rbs_large, we can tell the database to use it by issuing the following statement before our first change to data:

```
SET TRANSACTION USE ROLLBACK SEGMENT rbs_large;
```

LOCK TABLE

```
LOCK TABLE table_list IN lock_mode MODE [NOWAIT];
```

This statement bypasses the implicit database row-level locks by explicitly locking one or more tables in the specified mode. The *table_list* is a comma-delimited list of tables. The *lock_mode* is one of the following: ROW SHARE, ROW EXCLUSIVE, SHARE UPDATE, SHARE, SHARE ROW EXCLUSIVE, or EXCLUSIVE. The NOWAIT keyword specifies that the Oracle database should not wait for a lock to be released. If there is a lock when NOWAIT is specified, the database raises the exception "ORA-00054: resource busy and acquire with NOWAIT specified." The default database locking behavior is to wait indefinitely.

Autonomous Transactions

Autonomous transactions, often used for recording application log messages, execute within a block of code as separate transactions from the outer (main) transaction. Changes can be committed or rolled back in an autonomous transaction without committing or rolling back the main transaction. Changes committed in an autonomous transaction are visible to the main transaction, even though they occur after the start of the main transaction. Those changes committed in an autonomous transaction are visible to other transactions as well. The database suspends the main transaction while the autonomous transaction executes:

```
PROCEDURE main IS
BEGIN
   UPDATE ... -- Main transaction begins here
   DELETE ...
   at_proc;   -- Call the autonomous transaction
   SELECT ...
   INSERT ...
   COMMIT;    -- Main transaction ends here
END;

PROCEDURE at_proc IS
   PRAGMA AUTONOMOUS_TRANSACTION;
BEGIN          -- Main transaction suspends here
   SELECT ...
   INSERT ... -- Autonomous transaction begins here
   UPDATE ...
   DELETE ...
   COMMIT;
   /* Always commit or rollback at end of
      autonomous transaction. */
END; -- Main transaction resumes after closing
```

Changes made in the main transaction are not visible to the autonomous transaction, and if the main transaction holds any locks that the autonomous transaction waits for, a deadlock occurs. Using the NOWAIT option on UPDATE statements in autonomous transactions can help to minimize this kind of deadlock. Functions and procedures (local program, stand-alone, or packaged), database triggers, top-level anonymous PL/SQL blocks, and object methods can be declared autono-mous via the compiler directive PRAGMA AUTONO-MOUS_TRANSACTION. In addition, there must be a COM-MIT or a ROLLBACK at each exit point in the autonomous program.

Cursors in PL/SQL

Every SQL statement executed by the Oracle database has a pri-vate SQL area that contains information about the SQL state-ment and the set of data returned. In PL/SQL, a *cursor* is a name assigned to a specific private SQL area for a specific SQL statement. There can be either *static cursors*, whose SQL state-ment is determined at compile time, or *dynamic cursors*, whose SQL statement is determined at runtime.

Static cursors are used only for DML statements (SELECT, INSERT, UPDATE, DELETE, MERGE, or SELECT FOR UPDATE). These static cursors may be explicitly declared and named or may appear inline as implicit cursors.

Dynamic cursors are used for any type of valid SQL statement, including DDL (CREATE, TRUNCATE, ALTER) and DCL (GRANT, REVOKE). Dynamic cursors are typically imple-mented with the EXECUTE IMMEDIATE statement.

Explicit Cursors

Explicit cursors are SELECT statements that are declared explicitly in the declaration section of the current block or in a package specification. Use OPEN, FETCH, and CLOSE in the execution or exception sections of your programs.

Declaring explicit cursors

To use an explicit cursor, you must first declare it in the declaration section of a block or package. There are three types of explicit cursor declarations:

- A cursor without parameters; for example:

    ```
    CURSOR company_cur IS
        SELECT company_id FROM company;
    ```

- A cursor that accepts arguments through a parameter list; for example:

    ```
    CURSOR company_cur (id_in IN NUMBER) IS
        SELECT name FROM company
        WHERE company_id = id_in;
    ```

- A cursor header that contains a RETURN clause in place of the SELECT statement; for example:

    ```
    CURSOR company_cur (id_in IN NUMBER)
        RETURN company%ROWTYPE;
    ```

This last example shows that the "header" of a cursor can be declared separately from its implementation—which will then be found in the package *body*, as in:

```
PACKAGE BODY my_pkg
IS
    CURSOR company_cur (id_in IN NUMBER) IS
        SELECT * FROM company WHERE id = id_in;
END;
```

See "Packages" on page 129 for more information on package structure.

Opening explicit cursors

To open a cursor, you can use the following syntax:

```
OPEN cursor_name [(argument [,argument ...])];
```

where *cursor_name* is the name of the cursor as declared in the declaration section. The arguments are required if the definition of the cursor contains a parameter list, in which case you may use either positional notation, as above, and/or named notation:

```
OPEN cursor_name
    (parameter_name => argument [, ...]);
```

You must open an explicit cursor before you can fetch rows from that cursor. When the cursor is opened, the processing actually includes the parse, bind, open, and execute phases of SQL statement execution. This OPEN processing includes determining an execution plan, associating host variables and cursor parameters with the placeholders in the SQL statement, determining the result set, and, finally, setting the current row pointer to the first row in the result set.

When using a cursor FOR loop, the OPEN is implicit in the FOR statement. If you try to open a cursor that is already open, PL/SQL will raise an "ORA-06511: PL/SQL: cursor already open" exception.

Fetching from explicit cursors

The FETCH statement places the contents of the current row into local variables. To retrieve all rows in a result set, each row needs to be fetched. The syntax for a FETCH statement is:

```
FETCH cursor_name INTO
    { record | variable [, variable... ] };
```

where *cursor_name* is the name of the cursor as declared and opened.

Closing explicit cursors

After all rows have been fetched, a cursor needs to be closed. Closing a cursor enables the PL/SQL memory optimization algorithm to release the associated memory at an appropriate time. You can close an explicit cursor by specifying a CLOSE statement as follows:

```
CLOSE cursor_name;
```

where *cursor_name* is the name of the cursor declared and opened.

If you declare a cursor in a local anonymous, procedure, or function block, that cursor will close automatically when the block terminates. Package-based cursors must be closed explicitly, or they stay open for the duration of your session. Closing a cursor that is not open raises an INVALID_CURSOR exception.

Explicit cursor attributes

There are four attributes associated with cursors: ISOPEN, FOUND, NOTFOUND, and ROWCOUNT. These attributes can be accessed with the % delimiter to obtain information about the state of the cursor. The syntax for a cursor attribute is:

```
cursor_name%attribute
```

where *cursor_name* is the name of the explicit cursor.

The behaviors of the explicit cursor attributes are described in the following table:

Attribute	Description
%ISOPEN	TRUE if cursor is open FALSE if cursor is not open
%FOUND	NULL before the first fetch TRUE if record was fetched successfully FALSE if no row was returned INVALID_CURSOR if cursor isn't open
%NOTFOUND	NULL before the first fetch FALSE if record was fetched successfully TRUE if no row was returned INVALID_CURSOR if cursor isn't open
%ROWCOUNT	The number of rows fetched from the cursor INVALID_CURSOR if cursor isn't open

Frequently, a cursor attribute is checked as part of a loop that fetches rows from a cursor, as shown here:

```
DECLARE
    caller_rec caller_pkg.caller_cur%ROWTYPE;
BEGIN
    OPEN caller_pkg.caller_cur;
     LOOP
        FETCH caller_pkg.caller_cur into caller_rec;
        EXIT WHEN caller_pkg.caller_cur%NOTFOUND
                  OR
                  caller_pkg.caller_cur%ROWCOUNT > 10;

        UPDATE call
            SET caller_id = caller_rec.caller_id
            WHERE call_timestamp < SYSDATE;
    END LOOP;
    CLOSE caller_pkg.caller_cur;
END;
```

Implicit Cursors

Whenever a SQL statement is directly in the execution or exception section of a PL/SQL block, you are working with implicit cursors. SQL statements handled this way include INSERT, UPDATE, DELETE, MERGE, and SELECT INTO. Unlike explicit cursors, implicit cursors do not require separate statements to perform declaration, open, fetch, or close operations.

SELECT statements handle the %FOUND and %NOTFOUND attributes differently from the way that explicit cursors do. When an implicit SELECT statement does not return any rows, PL/SQL immediately raises the NO_DATA_FOUND exception, and control passes to the exception section. When an implicit SELECT returns more than one row, PL/SQL immediately raises the TOO_MANY_ROWS exception, and control passes to the exception section.

Implicit cursor attributes are referenced via the SQL cursor. For example:

```
BEGIN
   UPDATE activity SET last_accessed := SYSDATE
    WHERE UID = user_id;

   IF SQL%NOTFOUND THEN
       INSERT INTO activity_log (uid, last_accessed)
       VALUES (user_id, SYSDATE);
   END IF
END;
```

The following table lists the implicit cursor attributes:

Attributes	Description
SQL%ISOPEN	Always FALSE because the cursor is opened implicitly and closed immediately after the statement is executed.
SQL%FOUND	NULL before the statement. TRUE if one or more rows were inserted, merged, updated, or deleted, or if only one row was selected. FALSE if no row was selected, merged, updated, inserted, or deleted.
SQL %NOTFOUND	NULL before the statement. TRUE if no row was selected, merged, updated, inserted, or deleted. FALSE if one or more rows were inserted, merged, updated, or deleted.
SQL %ROWCOUNT	Number of rows affected by the cursor.
SQL%BULK_ ROWCOUNT	Pseudoassociative array (index-by table) containing the number of rows affected by the statements executed in bulk bind operations. See "Bulk Binds" on page 79 for more information.

Use the RETURNING clause in INSERT, UPDATE, and DELETE statements to obtain data modified by the associated DML statement. This clause allows you to avoid an additional SELECT statement to query the affected row after applying the

DML statement. Here is an example for the case that your DML affects exactly one row:

```
BEGIN
    UPDATE activity SET last_accessed := SYSDATE
    WHERE UID = user_id
            RETURNING last_accessed, cost_center
                INTO timestamp, chargeback_acct;
```

If your DML affects more than one row, you can use RETURN-ING BULK COLLECT to return all rows into collection variables. For example:

```
DECLARE
    TYPE date_array IS TABLE OF DATE;
    TYPE number_array IS TABLE OF NUMBER;
    dates date_array;
    nums number_array;
BEGIN
    UPDATE activity SET last_accessed := SYSDATE
        RETURNING last_accessed, cost_center
        BULK COLLECT INTO dates, nums;
```

SELECT FOR UPDATE clause

By default, the Oracle database locks rows as they are changed. To lock all rows in a result set, use the FOR UPDATE clause in your SELECT statement when you OPEN the cursor, instead of when you change the data. Using the FOR UPDATE clause does not require you to actually make changes to the data; it only locks the rows when opening the cursor. These locks are released on the next COMMIT or ROLLBACK. As always, these row locks do not affect other SELECT statements unless they, too, are FOR UPDATE. The FOR UPDATE clause is appended to the end of the SELECT statement and has the following syntax:

```
SELECT ...
    FROM ...
        FOR UPDATE [OF column_reference] [NOWAIT];
```

where *column_reference* is a comma-delimited list of columns that appear in the SELECT clause. The optional NOWAIT keyword means that if the program cannot obtain the locks immediately, Oracle will raise an ORA-00054 exception. In the absence of NOWAIT, the program will wait forever for any locks to be released.

In the following example, only columns from the inventory table are referenced FOR UPDATE, so no rows in the dog_breeds table are locked when hounds_in_stock_cur is opened:

```
DECLARE
    CURSOR hounds_in_stock_cur IS
        SELECT i.stock_no, i.breeder, d.size
          FROM dog_breeds d, inventory i
         WHERE d.breed = i.breed
           AND d.class = 'HOUND'
           FOR UPDATE OF i.stock_no, i.breeder;
```

WHERE CURRENT OF clause

UPDATE and DELETE statements in PL/SQL can use a WHERE CURRENT OF clause if they reference a cursor declared FOR UPDATE. This syntax indicates that the UPDATE or DELETE statement should modify the current row identified by the FOR UPDATE cursor. The syntax is:

```
[UPDATE | DELETE ] ...
    WHERE CURRENT OF cursor_name;
```

By using WHERE CURRENT OF, you do not have to repeat the WHERE clause in the SELECT statement. For example:

```
DECLARE
    CURSOR account_cur IS
        SELECT acct_no, enter_date FROM accounts
         WHERE enter_date < SYSDATE - 7
            FOR UPDATE;
BEGIN
    FOR account_rec IN wip_cur
    LOOP
```

```
        INSERT INTO acct_log (acct_no, order_date)
            VALUES (account_rec.acct_no
                , account_rec.enter_date);
        DELETE FROM accounts
            WHERE CURRENT OF account_cur;
    END LOOP;
END;
```

Native Dynamic SQL

Dynamic SQL is commonly implemented "natively" with the
EXECUTE IMMEDIATE statement together with the OPEN
FOR, FETCH, and CLOSE statements. The EXECUTE IMME-
DIATE statement is typically used for DDL, single-row
SELECTs, and other DML, while the OPEN FOR, FETCH, and
CLOSE statements support dynamic multirow queries. Here is
the syntax for these statements:

```
EXECUTE IMMEDIATE sql_statement
  [INTO {variable [,variable ...] |
        record | object}]
  [USING [IN | OUT | IN OUT] bind_argument
    [,[IN | OUT | IN OUT] bind_argument ...] ]
  [{RETURNING | RETURN}
      INTO bind_argument[,bind_argument]...];
```

The *sql_statement* is passed as an expression in the character
datatype family. Your *sql_statement* itself can be in a literal
string, VARCHAR2 variable, or even in a CLOB variable if the
statement length is greater than 32,767 bytes. The EXECUTE
IMMEDIATE statement parses and executes the SQL statement
in a single step. The EXECUTE IMMEDIATE statement
requires a terminating semicolon, but the *sql_statement* must
not have a trailing semicolon.[2]

---

2 Well, most statements, anyway. CREATE OR REPLACE statements
  and anonymous blocks do require semicolons.

Here is an example of executing a DDL statement inside PL/SQL:

```
EXECUTE IMMEDIATE 'TRUNCATE TABLE foo';
```

When designing your programs, keep in mind that executing DDL will automatically commit any pending transactions.

Next, an example with an UPDATE, which introduces the use of bind variable placeholders (recognizable because their names begin with a colon):

```
DECLARE
   new_sal NUMBER := 75000;
BEGIN
   sql_stmt :=
     'UPDATE emp SET salary = :new_sal
       WHERE emp_id = :empno';

   EXECUTE IMMEDIATE sql_stmt USING new_sal, 123;
```

At runtime, Oracle will positionally associate the values you supply in the USING clause with the bind variable placeholders. You can normally bind values only to variables in the dynamic PL/SQL block that have a SQL type. Beginning with Oracle Database 12c, however, you may also bind some PL/SQL-specific types such as record and collection types.

This bind variable syntax is needed only in the case that you are using dynamic SQL; when embedding static SQL into your program, any PL/SQL variables you reference in the statement automatically become bind variables. So the preceding example is for illustration purposes; it is the equivalent of the more straightforward:

```
DECLARE
   new_sal NUMBER := 75000;
BEGIN
   UPDATE emp SET salary = new_sal
     WHERE emp_id = 123;
```

If you have a dynamic query that will return multiple rows, you can use the OPEN FOR statement with a weakly-typed cursor variable. The rows are then fetched and the cursor closed:

```
DECLARE
    TYPE cv_typ IS REF CURSOR;
    cv cv_typ;
    laccount_no NUMBER;
    lbalance NUMBER;
BEGIN
    OPEN cv FOR
        'SELECT account_no, balance
           FROM accounts
          WHERE balance < 500';
    LOOP
        FETCH cv INTO laccount_no, lbalance;
        EXIT WHEN cv%NOTFOUND;
        -- Process the row...
    END LOOP;
    CLOSE cv;
END;
```

DBMS_SQL

For most dynamic SQL requirements, native dynamic SQL (NDS), illustrated in the preceding code block, is the easiest route to implementation and will likely perform the best. But Oracle's venerable DBMS_SQL package will be essential in the scenario where you have to deal with an unpredictable number of columns in the select-list or an unpredictable number of bind variables in the WHERE clause. This scenario is known in Oracle parlance as "method 4." [3]

The DBMS_SQL functions TO_REFCURSOR and TO_CUR-SOR_NUMBER allow you to switch back and forth between

---

[3] Oracle's reference documentation lists four different dynamic SQL scenarios, and labels them methods 1 through 4. Methods 1 through 3 are now commonly implemented with native dynamic SQL.

DBMS_SQL and native dynamic SQL, taking advantage of the best of both dynamic SQL techniques.

Please refer to the Oracle documentation, or to O'Reilly's *Oracle PL/SQL Programming*, for more details on using DBMS_SQL.

SQL Injection and Bind Variables

SQL injection is a security vulnerability that can occur with dynamic SQL when unintended (malicious) code is injected into a program's dynamic SQL statement. One important defense against SQL injection is to use bind variables. This technique is generally recommended, in any case, because SQL statements usually execute repeatedly, and bind variables reduce the need for parsing. Declare your dynamic cursor with placeholders for bind variables and then pass the bind arguments to the Oracle database at runtime with a USING clause. The parsed form of the statement will be reused from the shared pool, improving performance.

Bind variables cannot be used in any arbitrary part of a SQL statement; you still need to be conscious of SQL injection when designing programs that use dynamically constructed column names, WHERE clauses, table names, and the like. To learn more about securing PL/SQL from injection attacks, read the white paper entitled "How to write SQL injection proof PL/SQL," (*http://bit.ly/1NPg1mN*) available on the Oracle Technology Network.

Cursor Variables

A cursor variable is a data structure that points to a cursor object, which in turn points to the cursor's result set. You can use cursor variables to more easily retrieve rows in a result set from client and server programs. You also can use cursor variables to hide minor variations in queries.

The pattern for declaring a REF_CURSOR type and associated cursor variable is:

```
DECLARE
   TYPE ref_cursor_type_name IS REF CURSOR
      [RETURN record_type];
   cursor_variable ref_cursor_type_name;
```

If you do not include a RETURN type, you are declaring a *weakly-typed* REF CURSOR; variables of this type can be associated with any query at runtime. If you include the RETURN type, you're declaring a *strongly-typed* REF CURSOR; any cursor variable declared using that type can only FETCH INTO data structures that match the specified record type.

The advantage of using a strongly-typed REF CURSOR is that you get an early (compile-time) warning of any mismatch between the shape of the SQL statement and the destination variable. So use a weakly-typed REF CURSOR when you don't know the shape in advance.

The following code shows examples of declaration sections for weakly- and strongly-typed REF CURSORs:

```
1 DECLARE
2    -- Create type based on company table
3    TYPE company_ct IS REF CURSOR RETURN companies
%ROWTYPE;
4    company_cur company_ct;
5
6    -- And now the weak cursor:
7    TYPE any_ct IS REF CURSOR;
8    generic_curvar any_ct;
```

For weak cursors, you can use the built-in type SYS_REFCURSOR as a shortcut; lines 7 and 8 could be replaced with the more succinct:

```
generic_curvar SYS_REFCURSOR;
```

The syntax to OPEN a cursor variable is:

```
OPEN cursor_name FOR SELECT_statement;
```

You can FETCH and CLOSE a cursor variable using the same syntax as for explicit cursors.

There are several restrictions on cursor variables:

- You cannot declare package-level cursor variables because they do not have a persistent state. (You can declare them in packaged procedures and functions, however.)

- You cannot assign NULLs to a cursor variable nor can you use comparison operators to test for equality, inequality, or nullity.

- Neither database columns nor collections can store cursor variables.

- You cannot use remote procedure calls (RPCs) to pass cursor variables from one server to another.

Cursor Expressions

A cursor expression provides a way to return a nested cursor from within a query. The syntax for a cursor expression is:

```
CURSOR (subquery)
```

Cursor expressions can reduce the amount of redundant data returned to a calling program over techniques that involve joining the tables together. The cursor expression is opened automatically when the parent row is fetched. Cursor expressions can be nested as well. These nested cursors are closed when one of the following occurs:

- The nested cursor is explicitly closed by the program.

- The parent cursor is closed.

- The parent cursor is re-executed.

- An exception is raised during the fetch of the parent row.

An example of a cursor expression follows:

```
DECLARE
   CURSOR order_cur IS
```

```
       SELECT o.order_date ,o.order_status
            ,CURSOR(SELECT p.translated_name
                         ,i.unit_price
                         ,i.quantity
                     FROM oe.order_items i
                         ,oe.prod_descrips p
                    WHERE i.product_id = p.product_id
                      AND i.order_id = o.order_id)
       FROM oe.orders o
      WHERE order_date BETWEEN TO_DATE('01-Oct-15')
                          AND TO_DATE('31-Oct-15');
   odate    oe.orders.order_date%TYPE;
   ostatus  oe.orders.order_status%TYPE;
   od_cur   SYS_REFCURSOR;
   tname    oe.prod_descrips.translated_name%TYPE;
   price    oe.order_items.unit_price%TYPE;
   qty      oe.order_items.quantity%TYPE;
BEGIN
   OPEN order_cur;
   LOOP
      FETCH order_cur INTO odate, ostatus, od_cur;
      EXIT WHEN order_cur%NOTFOUND;
      LOOP
         FETCH od_cur INTO tname, price, qty;
         EXIT WHEN od_cur%NOTFOUND;
         DBMS_OUTPUT.PUT_LINE(odate||','||ostatus
             ||','||tname||','||price||','||qty);
      END LOOP;
   END LOOP;
   CLOSE order_cur;
END;
```

Exception Handling

PL/SQL allows developers to raise and handle errors (exceptions) in a very flexible and powerful way. Each PL/SQL block can have its own exception section in which exceptions can be trapped and handled (resolved or passed on to the enclosing block). When an exception is raised in a PL/SQL block, its execution section immediately terminates. Control is passed to the exception section. Every exception in PL/SQL has an error number and error message; some exceptions also have names.

Declaring Exceptions

Some exceptions have been predefined by Oracle in the STAN-DARD package or other built-in packages, such as UTL_FILE. See the following table for some of the most common predefined exceptions. You also can declare your own exceptions as follows:

```
exception_name EXCEPTION;
```

Error	Named exception
ORA-00001	DUP_VAL_ON_INDEX
ORA-00051	TIMEOUT_ON_RESOURCE
ORA-01001	INVALID_CURSOR
ORA-01012	NOT_LOGGED_ON
ORA-01017	LOGIN_DENIED
ORA-01403	NO_DATA_FOUND
ORA-01410	SYS_INVALID_ROWID
ORA-01422	TOO_MANY_ROWS
ORA-01476	ZERO_DIVIDE
ORA-01722	INVALID_NUMBER
ORA-06500	STORAGE_ERROR
ORA-06501	PROGRAM_ERROR
ORA-06502	VALUE_ERROR
ORA-06504	ROWTYPE_MISMATCH
ORA-06511	CURSOR_ALREADY_OPEN
ORA-06530	ACCESS_INTO_NULL
ORA-06531	COLLECTION_IS_NULL

Error	Named exception
ORA-06532	SUBSCRIPT_OUTSIDE_LIMIT
ORA-06533	SUBSCRIPT_BEYOND_COUNT
ORA-06548	NO_DATA_NEEDED
ORA-06592	CASE_NOT_FOUND
ORA-30625	SELF_IS_NULL

An exception can be declared only once in a block, but nested blocks can declare an exception with the same name as an outer block. If this multiple declaration occurs, scope takes precedence over name when handling the exception. The inner block's declaration takes precedence over a global declaration.

When you declare your own exception, you must RAISE it explicitly. All programmer-declared exceptions have an error code of 1 and the error message "User-defined exception," unless you use the EXCEPTION_INIT pragma.

You can associate an error number with a declared exception with the PRAGMA EXCEPTION_INIT statement using the following syntax:

```
DECLARE
    exception_name EXCEPTION;
    PRAGMA EXCEPTION_INIT
        (exception_name, error_number);
```

where *error_number* is a literal value (variable references are not allowed). This number can be an Oracle error, such as -955 (object exists), or an error in the user-definable range 20000 to -20999. For example, to execute the dynamic SQL in the variable sql_stmt, ignoring any ORA-00955 errors, run the following:

```
DECLARE
    ObjectExists EXCEPTION;
    PRAGMA EXCEPTION_INIT (ObjectExists, -955);
    sql_stmt VARCHAR2(100) :=
        'CREATE TABLE mydual AS SELECT * FROM dual';
```

```
BEGIN
    EXECUTE IMMEDIATE sql_stmt;
    -- Ignore ORA-955 errors (object already exists)
    EXCEPTION
        WHEN ObjectExists THEN NULL;
END;
```

Raising Exceptions

An exception can be raised in three ways:

- By the PL/SQL runtime engine
- By an explicit RAISE statement in your code
- By a call to the built-in function RAISE_APPLICA-TION_ ERROR

The syntax for the RAISE statement is:

```
RAISE [exception_name];
```

where *exception_name* is the name of an exception that you have declared, or an exception that is declared in the STAN-DARD package. If you use the RAISE statement inside an exception handler, you can omit the exception name to re-raise the current exception:

```
EXCEPTION
    WHEN exception_name
    THEN
            ...do_something;
            RAISE;
```

This syntax is not valid outside the exception section.

The RAISE_APPLICATION_ERROR built-in function has the following header:

```
RAISE_APPLICATION_ERROR (
    num BINARY_INTEGER,
    msg VARCHAR2,
    keeperrorstack BOOLEAN DEFAULT FALSE);
```

where *num* is the error number (an integer between -20999 and -20000), *msg* is the associated error message, and *keeperrorstack* defines whether your error adds to (TRUE), or replaces (FALSE), the existing errors on the stack.

Scope

The *scope* of an exception section is that portion of the code that is "covered" by the exception section. An exception handler will handle, or attempt to handle, only those exceptions that are raised in the executable section of its PL/SQL block. Exceptions raised in the declaration or exception sections are passed to the outer block automatically. Any line or set of PL/SQL code can be placed inside a BEGIN-END to define its own block and have its own exception section. This allows you to limit the propagation of an exception.

Propagation

Exceptions raised in a PL/SQL block propagate to an outer block if they are unhandled or re-raised in the exception section. When an exception occurs, PL/SQL looks for an exception handler that checks for the exception (or the WHEN OTHERS clause) in the current block. If a match is not found, PL/SQL propagates the exception to the enclosing block or calling program. This propagation continues until the exception is handled or propagated out of the outermost block, back to the calling program. In this case, the exception is "unhandled" and (1) stops the calling program, and (2) the host environment usually issues an automatic rollback of any outstanding transactions in that session.

Once an exception is handled, it will not propagate upward. If you want to trap an exception, display a meaningful error message, and have the exception propagate upward as an error, you must re-raise the exception. The RAISE statement can re-raise the current exception or raise a new exception, as shown here:

```
PROCEDURE delete_dept(deptno_in IN NUMBER)
IS
   still_have_employees EXCEPTION;
   PRAGMA EXCEPTION_INIT
      (still_have_employees, -2292);
BEGIN
   DELETE FROM dept
    WHERE deptno = deptno_in;
EXCEPTION
   WHEN still_have_employees
   THEN
      DBMS_OUTPUT.PUT_LINE
         ('Please delete employees in dept first');
      RAISE;  --Re-raise the current exception.
END;
```

WHEN OTHERS clause

Use the WHEN OTHERS clause in the exception handler as a catch-all to trap any exceptions that are not handled by specific WHEN clauses in the exception section. If present, this clause must be the last exception handler in the exception section. Specify this clause as follows:

```
EXCEPTION
   WHEN OTHERS
   THEN
      ...
```

Using WHEN OTHERS THEN NULL is generally considered poor programming practice; if you must employ a general-purpose exception handler, it should do something reasonable (e.g., log the error, alert operators, etc.) to avoid an application that silently ends with a failure.

SQLCODE and DBMS_UTILITY formatters for exception handlers

Inside any WHEN OTHERS section, you can use Oracle's built-ins, such as the SQLCODE function, and the various error and stack formatting tools. The former will enable your program to branch appropriately, while the latter will allow you to record the needed information about what went wrong. Prior to Oracle Database 12.1, you could use the functions in the DBMS_UTILITY package to return strings containing information about the execution call stack, error stack, and error backtrace, respectively:

```
CREATE TABLE err_test
    (widget_name    VARCHAR2(100)
    ,widget_count   NUMBER
    ,CONSTRAINT no_small_numbers CHECK
        (widget_count > 1000));

BEGIN
    INSERT INTO err_test (widget_name, widget_count)
    VALUES ('Athena',2);
EXCEPTION
    WHEN OTHERS THEN
        IF SQLCODE = -2290
            AND DBMS_UTILITY.FORMAT_ERROR_STACK LIKE
                '%NO_SMALL_NUMBERS%'
        THEN
            DBMS_OUTPUT.PUT_LINE (
                'Widget_count is too small.' );
        ELSE
            DBMS_OUTPUT.PUT_LINE(
                'Unhandled exception ' || SQLCODE);
            DBMS_OUTPUT.PUT_LINE(
                DBMS_UTILITY.FORMAT_CALL_STACK);
            DBMS_OUTPUT.PUT_LINE(
                DBMS_UTILITY.FORMAT_ERROR_BACKTRACE);
        END IF;
END;
```

This produces the following output:

Widget_count is too small.

In Oracle Database 12.1, a single package, UTL_CALL_STACK, provides that same information, plus much more fine-grained access to the contents of these formatted strings. Here, for example, is a block that utilizes the UTL_CALL_STACK API to obtain the fully qualified name of the *nested* subprogram that was executed:

```
FUNCTION call_stack_string RETURN VARCHAR2
IS
    l_subprogram  VARCHAR2 (32767);
    l_return      VARCHAR2 (32767);
BEGIN
    FOR indx IN REVERSE 2 ..
                    utl_call_stack.dynamic_depth
    LOOP
        l_subprogram :=
            utl_call_stack.concatenate_subprogram (
                utl_call_stack.subprogram (indx));
        l_return :=
            l_return || l_subprogram
            || ' ('
            || TO_CHAR
                (utl_call_stack.unit_line (indx))
            || ')';
    END LOOP;
    RETURN l_return;
END;
```

Please refer to Oracle documentation and O'Reilly's *Oracle PL/SQL Programming* for more details of this package.

There is another built-in function that provides error string information: SQLERRM. However, Oracle Corporation recommends that you limit use of this function to the SAVE EXCEPTIONS clause in FORALL statements.

Exceptions and transactions

When an exception is raised in a PL/SQL block, it does *not* instantly roll back your current transaction, even if the block issued an INSERT, UPDATE, or DELETE. If your exception handler catches the exception, you have control over what happens; for example, you may want to issue your own ROLLBACK statement.

If your exception goes unhandled (propagates out of the outermost block), however, most host environments, including SQL*Plus, will then force an automatic, unqualified rollback of any outstanding changes in your session.

Records in PL/SQL

A PL/SQL record is a data structure composed of multiple pieces of information called *fields*. To use a record, you must first define it and declare a variable of this type. There are three types of records: table-based, cursor-based, and programmer-defined.

Declaring Records

Define and declare records either in the declaration section of a PL/SQL block or globally, via a package specification.

You do not have to explicitly define table-based or cursor-based records, as they are implicitly defined with the same structure as a table or a cursor. Variables of these types are declared via the %ROWTYPE attribute. The record's fields correspond to the table's columns or the columns in the SELECT list.

```
DECLARE
   comp_rec   company%ROWTYPE;

   CURSOR comp_summary_cur IS
      SELECT c.company_id,SUM(s.gross_sales) gross
        FROM company c, sales s
       WHERE c.company_id = s.company_id;

   -- Declare a cursor-based record.
   comp_summary_rec   comp_summary_cur%ROWTYPE;
```

Programmer-defined records must be explicitly defined with the TYPE statement in the PL/SQL declaration section or in a package specification. Variables of this type then can be declared as shown here:

```
DECLARE
    TYPE name_rectype IS RECORD(
        prefix       VARCHAR2(15)
        ,first_name  VARCHAR2(30)
        ,middle_name VARCHAR2(30)
        ,sur_name    VARCHAR2(30)
        ,suffix      VARCHAR2(10) );

    TYPE employee_rectype IS RECORD (
        emp_id       NUMBER(10) NOT NULL
        ,mgr_id      NUMBER(10)
        ,dept_no     dept.deptno%TYPE
        ,title       VARCHAR2(20)
        ,name        name_rectype
        ,hire_date   DATE := SYSDATE
        ,fresh_out   BOOLEAN );

    -- Declare a variable of this type.
    new_emp_rec employee_rectype;
BEGIN
```

Referencing a Record's Fields

Individual fields are referenced via dot notation:

```
record_name.field_name
```

For example:

```
employee.first_name
```

Individual fields within a record can be read from or written to. They can appear on either the left or right side of the assignment operator:

```
BEGIN
    start_date := new_emp_rec.hire_date + 30;
```

```
new_emp_rec.fresh_out := FALSE;
...
```

Assigning Records

An entire record can be assigned to another record of the same type, but one record cannot be compared to another record via Boolean operators. This is a valid assignment:

```
shipto_address_rec := customer_address_rec
```

But this is not a valid comparison:

```
IF shipto_addr_rec = cust_addr_rec -- illegal
THEN
    ...
END IF;
```

The individual fields of the records need to be compared instead.

Values can be assigned to records or to the fields within a record in four different ways:

- You can use the assignment operator to assign a value to a field:

    ```
    new_emp_rec.hire_date := SYSDATE;
    ```

- You can SELECT INTO a whole record or the individual fields:

    ```
    SELECT emp_id, dept_id, hire_date
      INTO new_emp_rec
      FROM emp
     WHERE surname = 'LI'
    ```

- You can FETCH INTO a whole record or the individual fields:

    ```
    FETCH emp_cur INTO new_emp_rec;
    FETCH emp_cur
     INTO new_emp_rec.emp_id, new_emp_rec.name;
    ```

- You can assign all the fields of one record variable to another record variable of the same type:

```
IF rehire THEN
    new_emp_rec := former_emp_rec;
ENDIF;
```

This aggregate assignment technique works only for records declared with the same TYPE statement.

Records and DML

You insert into or update a database table using a %ROWTYPE record without having to specify each field individually in the following ways:

- Insert into a database table, using a %ROWTYPE record and the VALUES keyword:

```
DECLARE
    emp_rec  emp%ROWTYPE;
BEGIN
    emp_rec.empno := employees_seq.NEXTVAL;
    INSERT INTO emp VALUES (emp_rec);
END;
```

- Update a database table using a %ROWTYPE record and the SET ROW keywords:

```
FOR emp_rec IN emp_cur
LOOP
    change_record_values(emp_rec);

    UPDATE emp SET ROW = emp_rec
      WHERE empno = emp_rec.empno;
END LOOP;
```

These techniques allow you to write more compact code to interact with a database. If you are using Oracle Database 12*c* or higher, this approach also works with dynamic SQL, because bind variables can now be of a record datatype.

Nested Records

Nested records are records contained in fields that are records themselves. Nesting records is a powerful way to normalize data structures and hide complexity within PL/SQL programs. For example:

```
DECLARE
    -- Define a record.
    TYPE phone_rectype IS RECORD (
        area_code  VARCHAR2(3),
        exchange   VARCHAR2(3),
        phn_number VARCHAR2(4),
        extension  VARCHAR2(4));

    -- Define a record composed of records.
    TYPE contact_rectype IS RECORD (
        day_phone#  phone_rectype,
        eve_phone#  phone_rectype,
        cell_phone# phone_rectype);

    -- Declare a variable for the nested record.
    auth_rep_info_rec contact_rectype;
BEGIN
```

Collections in PL/SQL

There are three types of collections in PL/SQL: associative arrays (formerly known as index-by tables or PL/SQL tables), nested tables, and VARRAYs:

Associative arrays

Single-dimension, unbounded collections of homogeneous elements available only in PL/SQL, not in the Oracle database. Associative arrays are initially sparse; they have nonconsecutive subscripts. You can index by both integer and string, while nested tables and varrays can only be indexed by integer.

Nested tables

Single-dimension, unbounded collections of homogene-ous elements that can be declared within a PL/SQL block and also stored in the column of a table. Nested tables ini-tially are dense (they have consecutive subscripts), but they can become sparse through deletions.

VARRAYs

Variable-size arrays. Single-dimension, bounded collec-tions of homogeneous elements that can be declared within a PL/SQL block and also stored in the column of a table. VARRAYs are never sparse. Unlike nested tables, their element order is preserved when you store and retrieve them from the database.

The following table compares these similar collection types:

Characteristic	Associative array	Nested table	VARRAY
Dimensionality	Single	Single	Single
Usable in SQL?	Yes, as of Oracle Database 12c [a]	Yes	Yes
Usable as a column datatype in a table?	No	Yes; data stored "out of line" (in a separate table)	Yes; data typically stored "inline" (in the same table)
Uninitialized state	Empty (cannot be null); elements are undefined	Atomically null; illegal to reference elements	Atomically null; illegal to reference elements
Initialization	Automatic, when declared	Via constructor, fetch, assignment	Via constructor, fetch, assignment

Characteristic	Associative array	Nested table	VARRAY
In PL/SQL, elements referenced by	BINARY_INTEGER (−2,147,483,647 .. 2,147,483,647) or character string (VARCHAR2); maximum length of VARCHAR2 is 32,767, minimum length is 1	Positive integer between 1 and 2,147,483,647; elements cannot be referenced unless they have been initialized via the constructor or with the EXTEND function	Positive integer between 1 and 2,147,483,647; elements cannot be referenced unless they have been initialized via the constructor or with the EXTEND function
Sparse?	Yes	Initially no; after deletions, yes	No
Bounded?	No	Can be extended	Yes
Growing the number of elements in the collection	Assign a value to the element using a new subscript	Elements are added via the constructor or later via the EXTEND method	Elements are added via the constructor or later via the EXTEND method; however, you cannot EXTEND past the upper bound
Shrinking the size of the collection	Automatic	TRIM function	TRIM function
Can be compared for equality?	No	Yes (in Oracle Database 10*g* and later)	No

Characteristic	Associative array	Nested table	VARRAY
Elements retain ordinal position and subscript when stored and retrieved from the database	N/A; can't be stored in database	No	Yes

a SQL statements embedded in PL/SQL can use associative arrays via the TABLE operator (Oracle Database 12c and later).

Declaring a Collection

Collections are implemented as TYPEs. As with any programmer-defined type, you must first define the type; then you can declare instances of that type. The TYPE definition can be stored in the database or declared in the PL/SQL program. Each instance of the TYPE is a collection.

The syntax for declaring an associative array is:

```
TYPE type_name IS TABLE OF element_type [NOT NULL]
    INDEX BY {BINARY_INTEGER |
VARCHAR2(size_limit)};
```

The syntax for a nested table is:

```
[CREATE [OR REPLACE]] TYPE type_name { IS | AS }
TABLE OF
    element_type [NOT NULL];
```

The syntax for a VARRAY is:

```
[CREATE [OR REPLACE]] TYPE type_name { IS | AS }
{ VARRAY |
    VARYING ARRAY } (max_elements) OF element_type
    [NOT NULL];
```

The CREATE keyword defines the statement to be DDL and indicates that this type will exist in the database. The optional OR REPLACE keywords are used to rebuild an existing type, preserving the privileges. *type_name* is any valid identifier that will be used later to declare the collection. *max_elements* is the maximum size of the VARRAY. *element_type* is the type of the collection's elements. All elements are of a single type, which can be most scalar datatypes, an object type, or a REF object type. If the elements are objects, the object type itself cannot have an attribute that is a collection. Explicitly disallowed collection datatypes are BOOLEAN, NCHAR, NCLOB, NVARCHAR2, REF CURSOR, TABLE, and VARRAY.

NOT NULL indicates that a collection of this type cannot have any null elements. However, the collection can be atomically null (uninitialized).

Initializing a Collection

Initializing an associative array is not necessary—simply declaring it also initializes it. Initializing a nested table or a VARRAY can be done in any of three ways: explicitly with a constructor, implicitly with a fetch from the database, or implicitly with a direct assignment of another collection variable.

The constructor is a built-in function with the same name as the collection. It constructs the collection from the elements passed to it. The following example shows how you can create a nested table of colors and explicitly initialize it to three elements with a constructor:

```
DECLARE
   TYPE colors_tab_t IS TABLE OF VARCHAR2(30);
   colors_tab colors_tab_t :=
       colors_tab_t('RED','GREEN','BLUE');
BEGIN
```

The next example shows how you can create the nested table of colors and implicitly initialize it with a fetch from the database:

```
-- Create nested table in the database.
CREATE TYPE colors_tab_t IS TABLE OF VARCHAR2(32);

-- Create table with nested table type as column.
```

```
CREATE TABLE color_models
   (model_type    VARCHAR2(12)
   ,colors        colors_tab_t)
NESTED TABLE colors STORE AS
   color_model_colors_tab;

-- Add some data to the table.
INSERT INTO color_models
VALUES('RGB',colors_tab_t('RED','GREEN','BLUE'));

INSERT INTO color_models
   VALUES('CYMK'
          ,colors_tab_t('CYAN','YELLOW'
                        ,'MAGENTA' 'BLACK'));

-- Initialize collection of colors from table.
DECLARE
   basic_colors colors_tab_t;
BEGIN
   SELECT colors INTO basic_colors
     FROM color_models
    WHERE model_type = 'RGB';
END;
```

The third example shows how you can implicitly initialize the
table via an assignment from an existing collection:

```
DECLARE
   basic_colors Color_tab_t := Color_tab_t
      ('RED','GREEN','BLUE');
   my_colors Color_tab_t;
BEGIN
   my_colors := basic_colors;
   my_colors(2) := 'MUSTARD';
```

Adding and Removing Elements

Elements in an associative array can be added simply by refer-
encing new subscripts. To add elements to nested tables or
VARRAYs, you must first enlarge the collection with the
EXTEND function, and then you can assign a value to a new

element using one of the methods described in the previous section.

Use the DELETE function to remove an element in a nested table regardless of its position. The TRIM function also can be used to remove elements, but only from the end of a collection. To avoid unexpected results, do not use both DELETE and TRIM on the same collection.

Nested Table Functions

Several collection (multiset) functions can be used to manipulate collections. These are summarized in the following table. Note that COLLECT is valid only in a SQL statement; it cannot be used, for example, in a PL/SQL assignment.

Function	Return value	Description
=	BOOLEAN	Compares two nested tables and returns TRUE if they have the same named type and cardinality, and if the elements are equal.
<>	BOOLEAN	Compares two nested tables and returns FALSE if they differ in named type, cardinality, or equality of elements.
[NOT] IN ( )	BOOLEAN	Returns TRUE [FALSE] if the nested table to the left of IN exists in the list of nested tables specified in the parentheses.
CARDINALITY(x)	NUMBER	Returns the number of elements in VARRAY or nested table x. Returns NULL if the collection is atomically NULL (not initialized).
CAST(k AS t)	TYPE t	Changes the datatype of k to type t; used in conjunction with COLLECT or MULTISET.
COLLECT	NESTED TABLE	Used in conjunction with CAST to map a column to a collection.
MULTISET	NESTED TABLE	Used in conjunction with CAST to map a subquery to a collection.

Function	Return value	Description
x MULTISET EXCEPT [DISTINCT] y	NESTED TABLE	Performs a MINUS set operation on nested tables x and y, returning a nested table whose elements are in x, but not in y. The returned nested table, x, and y must all be of the same type. The DISTINCT keyword forces the elimination of duplicates from the returned nested table.
x MULTISET INTERSECT [DISTINCT] y	NESTED TABLE	Performs an INTERSECT set operation on nested tables x and y, returning a nested table whose elements are in both x and y. The returned nested table, x, and y must all be of the same type. The DISTINCT keyword forces the elimination of duplicates from the returned nested table.
x MULTISET UNION [DISTINCT] y	NESTED TABLE	Performs a UNION set operation on nested tables x and y, returning a nested table whose elements include all those in x as well as those in y. The returned nested table, x, and y must all be of the same type. The DISTINCT keyword forces the elimination of duplicates from the returned nested table.
SET(x)	NESTED TABLE	Returns nested table x without duplicate elements.
x IS [NOT] A SET	BOOLEAN	Returns TRUE [FALSE] if the nested table x is composed of unique elements.
x IS [NOT] EMPTY	BOOLEAN	Returns TRUE [FALSE] if the nested table x is empty.
e [NOT] MEMBER [OF] x	BOOLEAN	Returns TRUE [FALSE] if an expression e is a member of the nested table x.
y [NOT] SUBMULTISET [OF] x	BOOLEAN	Returns TRUE [FALSE] if the nested table y contains only elements that are also in the nested table x.

The CAST function works together with the COLLECT and MULTISET functions. MULTISET operates on a subquery. COLLECT operates on a column in a SQL statement:

```
CREATE TYPE email_list_t AS TABLE OF VARCHAR2(64);

-- COLLECT operates on a column
SELECT CAST(COLLECT(cust_email) AS email_list_t)
  FROM oe.customers;

-- which is equivalent to
SELECT CAST(
    MULTISET(
      SELECT cust_email
       FROM oe.customers)
    AS email_list_t)
FROM dual;
```

The following provides examples of the other nested table functions, operators, and expressions:

```
DECLARE
  TYPE nested_type IS TABLE OF NUMBER;
  nt1 nested_type := nested_type(1,2,3);
  nt2 nested_type := nested_type(3,2,1);
  nt3 nested_type := nested_type(2,3,1,3);
  nt4 nested_type := nested_type(1,2,4);
  answer nested_type;
BEGIN
  /* (1,2,3,1,2,4) */
  answer := nt1 MULTISET UNION nt4;
  /* (1,2,3,2,3,1,3) */
  answer := nt1 MULTISET UNION nt3;
  /* (1,2,3) */
  answer := nt1 MULTISET UNION DISTINCT nt3;
  /* (3,2,1) */
  answer := nt2 MULTISET INTERSECT nt3;
  /* (3,2,1) */
  answer := nt2 MULTISET INTERSECT DISTINCT nt3;
  /* (3) */
  answer := nt3 MULTISET EXCEPT nt2;
```

```
    /* ( ) */
    answer := nt3 MULTISET EXCEPT DISTINCT nt2;
    /* (2,3,1) */
    answer := SET(nt3);
    IF (nt1 IS A SET) AND (nt3 IS NOT A SET) THEN
        DBMS_OUTPUT.PUT_LINE(
            'nt1 has unique elements,
            but nt3 does not');
    END IF;
    IF (nt3 MULTISET EXCEPT DISTINCT nt2)
            IS EMPTY THEN
        DBMS_OUTPUT.PUT_LINE('empty set');
    END IF;
    IF 3 MEMBER OF (nt3 MULTISET EXCEPT nt2) THEN
        DBMS_OUTPUT.PUT_LINE('3 in answer set');
    END IF;
    IF nt1 SUBMULTISET nt3 THEN
        DBMS_OUTPUT.PUT_LINE('nt1 subset of nt3');
    END IF;
    IF SET(nt3) IN (nt1,nt2,nt3)  THEN
        DBMS_OUTPUT.PUT_LINE (
            'expression in list of nested tables');
    END IF;
END;
```

Collection Methods

Several built-in functions (methods) are defined for all collections. These methods are called with dot notation:

```
collection_name.method_name[(parameters)]
```

The methods are listed in the following table:

Collection method	Description
COUNT	A function. Returns the current number of elements in the collection. If a collection is atomically NULL, this method raises an exception. Consider the CARDINALITY( ) function instead.
DELETE [(i [, j])]	A procedure. Removes element i or elements i through j from a nested table or associative array. When called with no parameters, removes all elements in the collection. Reduces the COUNT if the element is not already DELETEd. Does not apply to VARRAYs.
EXISTS (i)	A function. Returns TRUE or FALSE to indicate whether element i exists. If the collection is an uninitialized nested table or VARRAY, returns FALSE.
EXTEND [(n [, i])]	A procedure. Appends n elements to a nested table or VARRAY, initializing them to the value of element i. Both i and n are optional, and n defaults to 1.
FIRST	A function. Returns the lowest index in use. Returns NULL when applied to empty initialized collections.
LAST	A function. Returns the greatest index in use. Returns NULL when applied to empty initialized collections.
LIMIT	A function. Returns the maximum number of allowed elements in a VARRAY. Returns NULL for associative arrays and nested tables.
PRIOR (i)	A function. Returns the index immediately before element i. Returns NULL if i is less than or equal to FIRST.
NEXT (i)	A function. Returns the index immediately after element i. Returns NULL if i is greater than or equal to LAST.
TRIM [(n)]	A procedure. Removes n elements at the end of the collection with the largest index. n is optional and defaults to 1. If n is NULL, TRIM does nothing. Associative arrays cannot be TRIMmed.

The EXISTS function returns a BOOLEAN, and all other functions and procedures return BINARY_INTEGER except for collections indexed by VARCHAR2, which can return character strings. All parameters are of the BINARY_INTEGER type.

Only EXISTS can be used on uninitialized nested tables or VARRAYs. Other methods applied to these atomically null collections will raise the COLLECTION_IS_NULL exception.

DELETE and TRIM both remove elements from a nested table, but TRIM also removes the placeholder, while DELETE does not. This behavior may be confusing because TRIM can remove previously DELETEd elements.

Here are examples of some collection methods in use with an associative array:

```
DECLARE
    TYPE population_type IS
        TABLE OF NUMBER INDEX BY VARCHAR2(64);
    continent_population population_type;
    howmany NUMBER;
    continent_name VARCHAR2(64);
BEGIN
    continent_population('Australia') := 30000000;
    -- Create new entry
    continent_population('Antarctica') := 1000;
    -- Replace old value
    continent_population('Antarctica') := 1001;
    continent_name := continent_population.FIRST;
    DBMS_OUTPUT.PUT_LINE (continent_name);
    DBMS_OUTPUT.PUT_LINE (
        continent_population(continent_name));
    continent_name := continent_population.LAST;
    DBMS_OUTPUT.PUT_LINE (continent_name);
    DBMS_OUTPUT.PUT_LINE
        (continent_population(continent_name));
END;
```

This example produces the following output:

```
Antarctica
1001
Australia
30000000
```

Here are examples of some collection methods in use with a nested table:

```
DECLARE
   TYPE colors_tab_t IS TABLE OF VARCHAR2(30);
   my_list colors_tab_t :=
      colors_tab_t('RED','GREEN','BLUE');
   element BINARY_INTEGER;
BEGIN
   DBMS_OUTPUT.PUT_LINE('my_list has '
      ||my_list.COUNT||' elements');
   my_list.DELETE(2); -- delete element two
   DBMS_OUTPUT.PUT_LINE('my_list has '
      ||my_list.COUNT||' elements');

   FOR element IN my_list.FIRST..my_list.LAST
   LOOP
      IF my_list.EXISTS(element)
      THEN
         DBMS_OUTPUT.PUT_LINE(my_list(element)
            || ' Prior= '||my_list.PRIOR(element)
            || ' Next= ' ||my_list.NEXT(element));
      ELSE
         DBMS_OUTPUT.PUT_LINE('Element '|| element
            ||' deleted. Prior=
               '||my_list.PRIOR(element)
            || ' Next= '||my_list.NEXT(element));
      END IF;
   END LOOP;
END;
```

This example produces the following output:

```
my_list has 3 elements
my_list has 2 elements
RED Prior=  Next= 3
Element 2 deleted. Prior= 1 Next= 3
BLUE Prior= 1 Next=
```

Collections and Privileges

As with other TYPEs in the database, you need the EXECUTE privilege on that TYPE to use a collection type created by another schema (user account) in the database. You can use synonyms for user-defined TYPE names.

Nested Collections

Nested collections are collections contained in members that are collections themselves. Nesting collections is a powerful way to implement object-oriented programming constructs within PL/SQL programs. For example:

```
CREATE TYPE books IS TABLE OF VARCHAR2(64);
CREATE TYPE our_books IS TABLE OF books;
```

Bulk Binds

You can use collections to improve the performance of SQL operations executed iteratively by using *bulk binds*. Bulk binds reduce the number of context switches between the PL/SQL engine and the SQL engine. Two PL/SQL language constructs implement bulk binds: FORALL and BULK COLLECT INTO.

The syntax for the FORALL statement is:

```
FORALL bulk_index IN [lower_bound..upper_bound
  | INDICES OF collection_variable[BETWEEN
lower_bound AND upper_bound]
  | VALUES OF collection_variable ]
  [SAVE EXCEPTIONS]
  sql_statement;
```

bulk_index can be used only in the *sql_statement* and only as a collection index (subscript). When PL/SQL processes this statement, the whole collection—instead of each individual collection element—is sent to the database server for processing. To delete all the accounts in the collection named inactives from the table ledger, do this:

```
FORALL i IN inactives.FIRST..inactives.LAST
    DELETE FROM ledger WHERE acct_no = inactives(i);
```

If nonconsecutive index values result from deletions, you will need to use the INDICES OF syntax to skip over the deleted elements:

```
FORALL i IN INDICES OF inactives
    DELETE FROM ledger WHERE acct_no = inactives(i);
```

If you are interested in the values of a sparse collection of integers instead of the indices, you will need to use the VALUES OF syntax:

```
FORALL i IN VALUES OF inactives_list
    DELETE FROM ledger WHERE acct_no = inactives(i);
```

The INDICES OF and VALUES OF keywords allow you to specify a subset of rows in a driving collection that will be used in the FORALL statement. To match the row numbers in the data collection with the row numbers in the driving collection, use the INDICES OF clause. To match the row numbers in the data collection with the values found in the defined rows of the driving collection, use the VALUES OF clause.

The default is for the database to stop after the first exception encountered. Specify SAVE EXCEPTIONS to indicate that processing should continue after encountering exceptions. The cursor attribute %BULK_EXCEPTIONS stores a collection of records containing the errors. These records have two fields, EXCEPTION_INDEX and EXCEPTION_CODE, which contain the FORALL iteration (during which the exception was raised) as well as the SQLCODE for the exception. If no exceptions are raised, the SQL%BULK_EXCEPTIONS.COUNT method returns 0. For example:

```
DECLARE
    TYPE NameList IS TABLE OF VARCHAR2(32);
    name_tab NameList := NameList(
            'Dawes','Feuerstein','Gennick'
            ,'Pribyl','Beresniewicz','Dawes','Dye');
    error_count NUMBER;
```

```
      bulk_errors EXCEPTION;
      PRAGMA exception_init(bulk_errors, -24381);
   BEGIN
      FORALL indx IN name_tab.FIRST..name_tab.LAST
         SAVE EXCEPTIONS
         INSERT INTO authors (name) VALUES
            (name_tab(indx));
   EXCEPTION
      WHEN OTHERS
      THEN
         error_count := SQL%BULK_EXCEPTIONS.COUNT;
         DBMS_OUTPUT.PUT_LINE
            ('Number of errors is ' || error_count);
         FOR indx IN 1..error_count
         LOOP
            DBMS_OUTPUT.PUT_LINE('Error ' || indx ||
               ' occurred during iteration ' ||
               SQL%BULK_EXCEPTIONS(indx).ERROR_INDEX);
            DBMS_OUTPUT.PUT_LINE('Error is ' ||
               SQLERRM (
                  -SQL%BULK_EXCEPTIONS(indx).
                     ERROR_CODE));
         END LOOP;
   END;

   Number of errors is 2
   Error 1 occurred during iteration 5
   Error is ORA-00001: unique constraint (.) violated
   Error 2 occurred during iteration 7
   Error is ORA-00001: unique constraint (.) violated
```

Moving along to the second bulk approach, BULK COLLECT
INTO:

```
BULK COLLECT INTO collection_name_list;
```

where *collection_name_list* is a comma-delimited list of collections, one for each column in the SELECT.

The BULK COLLECT INTO clause can be used in SELECT
INTO, FETCH INTO, or RETURNING INTO statements. For
example:

```
DECLARE
   TYPE name_tab IS TABLE OF vendors.name%TYPE;
   TYPE term_tab IS TABLE OF vendors.terms%TYPE;
   v_names name_tab;
   v_terms term_tab;
BEGIN
   SELECT name, terms
     BULK COLLECT INTO v_names, v_terms
     FROM vendors
    WHERE terms < 30;
   ...
END;
```

If you use Oracle Database 12c or later, you can use SQL's
FETCH FIRST clause to get top-N results; the preceding
SELECT statement could become:

```
SELECT name, terms
  BULK COLLECT INTO v_names, v_terms
  FROM vendors
 ORDER BY terms, name
 FETCH FIRST 50 ROWS ONLY;
```

And, if your application needs to "paginate" the results, combine FETCH FIRST with the OFFSET clause:

```
PROCEDURE fetch_search_results
   (p_page# IN INTEGER DEFAULT 1)
IS
   c_lines CONSTANT INTEGER := 50;
   v_offset INTEGER := c_lines * (p_page# - 1);
BEGIN
   SELECT name, terms
     BULK COLLECT INTO v_names, v_terms
     FROM vendors
    ORDER BY terms, name
   OFFSET v_offset ROWS
      FETCH NEXT c_lines ROWS ONLY;
   ...
```

The next example deletes products in an input list of categories, and the SQL RETURNING clause returns a list of deleted products:

```
FUNCTION cascade_category_delete (
   categorylist clist_t) RETURN prodlist_t
IS
   prodlist prodlist_t;
BEGIN
   FORALL aprod IN categorylist.FIRST ..
                   categorylist.LAST
      DELETE FROM product
       WHERE product_id IN categorylist(aprod)
       RETURNING product_id
          BULK COLLECT INTO prodlist;
   RETURN prodlist;
END;
```

You can use the SQL%BULK_ROWCOUNT cursor attribute for bulk bind operations. It is like an associative array containing the number of rows affected by the executions of the bulk bound statements. The nth element of SQL%BULK_ROWCOUNT contains the number of rows affected by the nth execution of the SQL statement. For example:

```
FORALL i IN inactives.FIRST..inactives.LAST
   DELETE FROM ledger WHERE acct_no = inactives(i);

FOR counter IN inactives.FIRST..inactives.LAST
LOOP
   IF SQL%BULK_ROWCOUNT(counter) = 0
   THEN
      DBMS_OUTPUT.PUT_LINE(
         'No rows deleted for '|| counter);
   END IF;
END LOOP;
```

You cannot pass SQL%BULK_ROWCOUNT as a parameter to another program or use an aggregate assignment to another collection. The value of %ROWCOUNT is the sum of all %BULK_ROWCOUNT elements. Attributes %FOUND and

%NOTFOUND reflect only the last execution of the SQL statement.

Built-in Functions and Packages

Oracle Corporation supplies many built-in functions and packages. The following sections describe some of the more commonly used built-ins.

Built-in Functions

The Oracle database provides dozens of built-in functions. Although most of these functions are available to both SQL and PL/SQL, there are some notable exceptions. The DECODE function, for example, is not available to PL/SQL except within SQL statements included in your PL/SQL programs. The *Oracle Database SQL Reference* contains implementation details for the many functions of PL/SQL with the package STANDARD. You can view this package specification within the file *stdspec.sql* located in the *ORACLE_HOME/rdbms/admin* directory on the database server.

Conversion functions

Built-in function	Description
ASCIISTR(*string*)	Converts *string* in any character set to the ASCII version of *string* in the database character set.
CAST(*expression* AS *datatype*)	Converts *expression* to type *datatype*. (Use as a powerful substitute for TO_DATE.)
CHARTOROWID(*string*)	Converts *string* to a ROWID datatype.
CONVERT(*string*, *destination_character_set*, *source_character_set*)	Converts *string* from the source character set to the destination character set. (The default source character set is the database character set.)

Built-in function	Description
FROM_TZ(*timestamp_value, time_zone*)	Adds time zone information to a TIMESTAMP value (converting it to a TIMESTAMP WITH TIME ZONE value).
HEXTORAW(*string*)	Converts *string* containing hexadecimal characters to its raw equivalent.
MULTISET	Maps a database table to a collection.
NUMTODSINTERVAL(*n, interval_unit*)	Converts numeric expression *n* to an INTERVAL DAY TO SECOND literal; *interval_unit* can be DAY, HOUR, MINUTE, or SECOND.
NUMTOYMINTERVAL(*n, interval_unit*)	Converts numeric expression *n* to an INTERVAL YEAR TO MONTH literal; *interval_unit* can be YEAR or MONTH.
RAWTOHEX(*raw*)	Converts *raw* value to its hexadecimal equivalent.
REFTOHEX(*ref*)	Converts *ref* expression into a string containing its hexadecimal equivalent.
ROWIDTOCHAR(*rowid*)	Converts *rowid* to a VARCHAR2(18) string equivalent.
ROWIDTONCHAR(*rowid*)	Converts *rowid* to an NVARCHAR2(18) string equivalent.
TABLE	Maps a collection to a database table (inverse of MULTISET).
TO_BINARY_FLOAT(*expression* [*,fmt*])	Converts number or string *expression* to a BINARY_FLOAT; optionally use format model *fmt*.
TO_BINARY_DOUBLE(*expression* [*,fmt*])	Converts number or string *expression* to a BINARY_DOUBLE; optionally use format model *fmt*.

Built-in function	Description
TO_CHAR, TO_NCHAR(*expression* [,*fmt*])	Converts *expression* to a string (VARCHAR2 or NVARCHAR2, respectively); optionally use format model *fmt*.
TO_CLOB, TO_NCLOB(*c*)	Converts *c* from a VARCHAR2, NVARCHAR2, or NCLOB value to a CLOB (or NCLOB).
TO_DATE(*expression* [,*fmt*])	Converts string *expression* to a DATE datatype; optionally use format model *fmt*.
TO_DSINTERVAL(*string*)	Converts character *string* of a CHAR, VARCHAR2, NCHAR, or NVARCHAR2 datatype to an INTERVAL DAY TO SECOND type.
TO_LOB(*c*)	Converts *c* from a LONG or LONG RAW to a LOB.
TO_MULTI_BYTE(*string*)	Where possible, converts single-byte characters in the input *string* to their multibyte equivalents.
TO_NUMBER(*expression* [,*fmt*])	Converts string or numeric (such as a BINARY_FLOAT) *expression* to a NUMBER; optionally use format model *fmt*.
TO_RAW(*b*)	Converts *b* from a BLOB to a RAW.
TO_SINGLE_BYTE(*string*)	Converts multibyte characters in *string* to their corresponding single-byte characters.
TO_TIMESTAMP(*expression* [,*fmt*])	Converts string *expression* to a value of type TIMESTAMP; optionally use format model *fmt*.
TO_TIMESTAMP_TZ(*expression* [,*fmt*])	Converts string *expression* to a value of type TIMESTAMP WITH TIMEZONE; optionally use format model *fmt*.
TO_YMINTERVAL(*string*)	Converts character *string* of a CHAR, VARCHAR2, NCHAR, or NVARCHAR2 datatype to an INTERVAL YEAR TO MONTH type.

Built-in function	Description
TRANSLATE ... USING(string USING CHAR_CS)	Converts string between the database character set and the national character set. Used for ANSI compatibility; mimics TO_CHAR or TO_NCHAR functionality.
UNISTR(string)	Translates string containing Unicode encoding values (e.g., x00e5) to a Unicode string literal in the database Unicode character set.

String functions

Built-in function	Description
ASCII(string)	Returns the numeric code in the database character set representing the first character in string.
ASCIISTR(string)	Takes a string in any character set and converts it into a string of ASCII characters. Any non-ASCII characters are represented using \XXXX Unicode notation.
CHR(code_location)	Inverse of ASCII function; returns a VARCHAR2 character of length 1 that corresponds to the location in the collating sequence provided as a parameter. A variation of CHR is useful when working with national character set data.
CHR(code_location USING NCHAR_CS)	Returns an NVARCHAR2 character from the national character set.
COMPOSE(string)	Takes a Unicode string as input and returns that string in its fully normalized form.
CONCAT(string1, string2)	Appends string2 to the end of string1.

Built-in function	Description
CONVERT(*string, target_char_set* [, *source_char_set*])	Converts a *string* from one character set to another. Default source is the database character set.
DECOMPOSE(*string* [CANONICAL])	Takes a Unicode *string* as input and returns that string with any precomposed characters decomposed into their separate elements. CANONICAL optionally gives a result that may be reversed using COMPOSE.
GREATEST(*string1, string2, ...*)	Takes one or more *strings* as input and returns the string that would come last (i.e., sorts highest) if the inputs were sorted in ascending order. Compare to LEAST.
INITCAP(*string*)	Reformats the case of the *string* argument, setting the first letter of each word to uppercase and the remainder of the letters to lowercase. A word is a set of characters separated by a space or nonalphanumeric character (such as # or _). For example, INITCAP('this is lower') gives 'This Is Lower'.
INSTR(*string1, string2* [[, *start_position*], *nth*])	Returns the position at which *string2* is found within *string1*; otherwise, returns 0. *start_position* defines the starting position and defaults to 1 if not present. With a negative *start_position*, searching begins at the end of *string1* and works backward. *nth* defines the ordinal occurrence (1st, 2nd, 3rd, etc.) of *string2* in *string1*, and defaults to 1 if not present.

Built-in function	Description
LEAST(string1, string2, ...)	Takes one or more *strings* as input and returns the string that would come first (i.e., the least) if the inputs were sorted in ascending order. Compare to GREATEST.
LENGTH(string)	Returns the number of characters in a *string*. The variations LENGTHB, LENGTHC, LENGTH2, and LENGTH4 return the number of bytes, the number of Unicode characters, the number of USC2 code points, and the number of USC4 code points, respectively. LENGTH returns NULL when passed a NULL, and zero when passed a zero length (but non-NULL) CLOB.
LOWER(string)	Converts all letters in the specified *string* to lowercase (the inverse of UPPER).
LPAD(string, padded_length [,pad_string])	Returns the value from *string*, but padded on the left with enough *pad_string* characters to make the result *padded_length* characters long. *pad_string* defaults to a space if not present.
LTRIM(string [,trim_string])	Removes, or trims, any characters found in *trim_string* from the leading edge of *string*. *trim_string* defaults to a space if not present. (See also TRIM [ISO standard] and RTRIM.)

Built-in function	Description
NCHR(*code_location*)	Returns an NVARCHAR2 character (length 1) that corresponds to the location in the national character set collating sequence specified by *code_location*. (Provides the same functionality as the CHR function's USING NCHAR_CS clause.)
NLS_INITCAP(*string*)	Returns a version of *string* (which should be of type NVARCHAR2 or NCHAR), setting the first letter of each word to uppercase and the remainder to lowercase. The return value is a VARCHAR2. A word is a set of characters separated by a space or nonalphanumeric character.
NLS_INITCAP(*string*, 'NLS_SORT=*sort_sequence_name*')	You may specify a linguistic sorting sequence that affects the definition of "first letter," as in the preceding built-in function. For *sort_sequence_name*, specify a linguistic sort name as described in the *Oracle Database Globalization Support Guide*.
NLS_LOWER(*string*) and NLS_LOWER(*string*, 'NLS_SORT=*sort_sequence_name*')	Lowercases a *string* in accordance with language-specific rules. (See NLS_INITCAP for how NLS_SORT can affect the results.)
NLS_UPPER(*string*) and NLS_UPPER(*string*, 'NLS_SORT=*sort_sequence_name*')	Uppercases a *string* in accordance with language-specific rules. (See NLS_INITCAP for how NLS_SORT can affect the results.)

Built-in function	Description
NLSSORT(*string*) and NLSSORT(*string*, 'NLS_SORT=*sort_sequence_name*')	Returns a *string* of bytes that can be used to sort a string value in accordance with language-specific rules. The string returned is of the RAW datatype.
REGEXP_INSTR, REGEXP_LIKE, REGEXP_REPLACE, REGEXP_SUBSTR	See "Built-in Regular Expression Functions" on page 99 for descriptions.
REPLACE(*string, match_string, replace_string*)	Returns a *string* in which all occurrences of *match_string* in *string* are replaced by *replace_string*. Use REPLACE to search for a pattern of characters and then change all instances of that pattern in a single function call.
RPAD(*string, padded_length[,pad_string]*)	Returns *string* padded on the right with enough *pad_string* occurrences to make the result *padded_length* characters long. *pad_string* defaults to a space.
RTRIM(*string [,trim_string]*)	Removes, or trims, any *trim_string* characters from the right, or trailing edge, of *string*. (See also TRIM [ISO standard] and LTRIM.) *trim_string* defaults to a space.
SOUNDEX(*string*)	Returns a string that is the "phonetic representation" of *string* (via algorithm defined by Donald E. Knuth).

Built-in function	Description
SUBSTR(*string, start,* [*length*])	Returns a substring from *string*, beginning with the character at position *start* and going for *length* characters. If *start* is negative, the beginning position is counted from the end of the string rather than the beginning. *length* defaults to the remainder of *string*.
TO_CHAR(*national_character_data*)	Converts data in the national character set to its equivalent representation in the database character set. (See also TO_NCHAR.) You can also use TO_CHAR to convert date and time values, as well as numbers, into strings.
TO_MULTI_BYTE(*string*)	Translates single-byte characters to their multibyte equivalents (the inverse of TO_SINGLE_BYTE).
TO_NCHAR(*database_character_data*)	Converts data in the database character set to its equivalent representation in the national character set. (See also TO_CHAR and TRANSLATE...USING.)
TO_SINGLE_BYTE(*string*)	Translates multibyte characters to their single-byte equivalents (the inverse of TO_MULTI_BYTE).
TRANSLATE (*string, search_set, replace_set*)	Replaces every instance in *string* of a character from *search_set* with the corresponding character from *replace_set*.

Built-in function	Description
TRANSLATE(*text* USING CHAR_CS) and TRANSLATE(*text* USING NCHAR_CS)	Translates character data to either the database character set (CHAR_CS) or the national character set (NCHAR_CS). The output datatype will be either VARCHAR2 or NVARCHAR2, depending on whether you are converting to the database or the national character set, respectively.
TRIM ([[LEADING | TRAILING | BOTH] *trim_character* FROM] *string*)	Returns a version of *string* that omits any leading and trailing spaces. The optional keywords LEADING FROM, TRAILING FROM, and BOTH FROM cause the trimming of only leading, trailing, or both (the default) leading and trailing *trim_character*s. *trim_character* defaults to a space.
UNISTR(*string*)	Returns *string* converted into Unicode (the inverse of ASCISTR). You can represent nonprintable characters in the input *string* using \XXXX Unicode notation.
UPPER(*string*)	Returns a version of *string* with all letters made uppercase.

Numeric functions

Built-in function	Description
ABS(*n*)	Returns the absolute value of *n*.
ACOS(*n*)	Returns the arc cosine of *n*, where *n* must be between π and 1. The returned value is between 0 and π.
ASIN(*n*)	Returns the arc sine, where *n* must be between −1 and 1. The returned value is between $-\pi/2$ and $\pi/2$.

Built-in function	Description
ATAN(n)	Returns the arc tangent, where the number n must be between −infinity and infinity. The returned value is between $-\pi/2$ and $\pi/2$.
ATAN2(n, m)	Returns the arc tangent of n/m, where the numbers n and m must be between −infinity and infinity. The returned value is between $-\pi$ and π. The result of ATAN2(n,m) is defined to be identical to ATAN(n/m).
BIN_TO_NUM(b1, b2,...bn)	Converts the bit vector represented by b1 through bn into a number. Each of b1 through bn must evaluate to either 0 or 1.
BITAND(n, m)	Performs a logical AND between n and m.
CEIL(n)	Returns the smallest integer greater than or equal to n.
COS(n)	Returns the cosine of the angle n, which must be expressed in radians.
COSH(n)	Returns the hyperbolic cosine of n. If n is a real number, and i is the imaginary square root of −1, then the relationship between COS and COSH can be expressed as follows: COS (i * n) = COSH (n).
EXP(n)	Returns the value e raised to the nth power, where n is the input argument. The number e (approximately equal to 2.71828) is the base of the system of natural logarithms.
FLOOR(n)	Returns the largest integer that is less than or equal to n.
GREATEST(n1, n2,...n3)	Returns the highest ordinal element from a list of input numbers.
LEAST(n1, n2,...n3)	Returns the lowest ordinal element from a list of input numbers.
LN(n)	Returns the natural logarithm of n. The argument n must be greater than or equal to 0.
LOG(b, n)	Returns the base b logarithm of n. The argument n must be greater than or equal to 0. The base b must be greater than 1.

Built-in function	Description
MOD(n, m)	Returns the remainder of n divided by m. The remainder is computed using a formula equivalent to $n-(m*FLOOR(n/m))$ when n and m are both positive or both negative, and $n-(m*CEIL(n/m))$ when the signs of n and m differ.
NANVL(n, m)	Returns m if n is NaN (not a number); otherwise, returns n. The value returned will be in the type of the argument with the highest numeric precedence: BINARY_DOUBLE, BINARY_FLOAT, or NUMBER, in that order.
POWER(n, m)	Raises n to the power m. If n is negative, then m must be an integer.
REMAINDER(n, m)	Returns the remainder of n divided by m. The remainder is defined as follows: $n-(m*ROUND(n/m))$.
ROUND(n)	Returns n rounded to the nearest integer.
ROUND(n, m)	Returns n rounded to m decimal places. The value of m can be less than zero. A negative value for m directs ROUND to round digits to the left of the decimal point rather than to the right.
SIGN(n)	Returns -1, 0, or $+1$, depending on whether n is less than zero, equal to zero, or greater than zero.
SIN(n)	Returns the sine of the specified angle, which must be expressed in radians.
SINH(n)	Returns the hyperbolic sine of n. If n is a real number, and i is the imaginary square root of -1, then the relationship between SIN and SINH can be expressed as follows: $SIN(i*n)=i*SINH(n)$.
SQRT(n)	Returns the square root n, which must be greater than or equal to 0.
TAN(n)	Returns the tangent of the angle n, which must be expressed in radians.

Built-in function	Description
TANH(*n*)	Returns the hyperbolic tangent of *n*. If *n* is a real number, and *i* is the imaginary square root of −1, then the relationship between TAN and TANH can be expressed as follows: TAN (*i* * *n*) = *i* * TANH (*n*).
TRUNC(*n* [, *p*])	Truncates *n* to *m* decimal places. The optional precision *p* defaults to 0 and, if negative, truncates (zeros out) *p* places to left of the decimal.

Date and time functions

Built-in function	Description
ADD_MONTHS(*date*, *n*)	Adds *n* months to *date*, returning a DATE.
CAST({ *expression* | MULTISET(*subquery*) } AS *type*)	Converts a value from one datatype or collection type to another. Use the MULTISET keyword when casting to a collection type.
CURRENT_DATE	Returns the current date and time as a DATE value in the session time zone.
CURRENT_TIMESTAMP(*p*)	Returns the current date and time as a TIMESTAMP WITH TIME ZONE value in the session time zone. The optional precision *p* specifies the subsecond number of digits to the right of the decimal and defaults to 6.
DBTIMEZONE	Returns the time zone offset (from UTC) of the database time zone in the form of a character string in format [+|-]HH24:MI; for example, -05:00.
EXTRACT(*element* FROM *expression*)	Returns the value of a specific datetime element from the datetime expression. The element can be one of YEAR, MONTH, DAY, HOUR, MINUTE, SECOND, TIMEZONE_HOUR, TIMEZONE_MINUTE, TIMEZONE_REGION, or TIMEZONE_ABBR.

Built-in function	Description
FROM_TZ(*ts, tz*)	Adds time zone *tz* to TIMESTAMP *ts*, converting it to a TIMESTAMP WITH TIME ZONE.
LAST_DAY(*expression*)	Returns the last day in the month containing the DATE *expression*.
LOCALTIMESTAMP(*p*)	Returns the current date and time as a TIMESTAMP value in the local time zone. The optional precision *p* specifies the subsecond number of digits to the right of the decimal.
MONTHS_BETWEEN(*end_date, start_date*)	Calculates the number of months between *start_date* and *end_date*.
NEW_TIME(*date,tz1,tz2*)	Translates the date value from time zone *tz1* to *tz2*. Included for backward compatibility; consider using a TIMESTAMP WITH TIMEZONE datatype instead.
NEXT_DAY(*date,dow*)	Returns the DATE of the first *dow* weekday that is later than *date*.
NUMTODSINTERVAL(*n, unit*)	Converts number *n* representing *unit* number to a value of type INTERVAL DAY TO SECOND. *unit* can be one of DAY, HOUR, MINUTE, or SECOND.
NUMTOYMINTERAL(*n, unit*)	Converts number *n* representing *unit* number to a value of type INTERVAL YEAR TO MONTH. *unit* can be one of YEAR or MONTH.
ROUND(*date, fmt*)	Returns *date* rounded to the optional format model *fmt* level of granularity. If *fmt* is not specified, *date* is rounded to the nearest day.
SESSIONTIMEZONE	Returns the time zone offset (from UTC) of the session time zone in the form of a character string.
SYSDATE	Returns the current date and time from the Oracle database server as a DATE value.

Built-in function	Description
SYS_EXTRACT_UTC(*dt*)	Converts the TIMESTAMP WITH TIME ZONE value *dt* to a TIMESTAMP having the same date and time, but normalized to UTC.
SYSTIMESTAMP	Returns the current date and time from the Oracle database server as a TIMESTAMP WITH TIME ZONE value.
TO_CHAR(*dt, fmt*)	Converts the datetime *dt* to a string using optional format model *fmt*, which defaults to the session NLS_DATE_FORMAT.
TO_DATE(*string, fmt*)	Converts *string* to a DATE; optionally use format model *fmt*, which defaults to the session NLS_DATE_FORMAT.
TO_DSINTERVAL(*string*)	Converts the character string representation of an interval expressed in days, hours, minutes, and seconds to a value of INTERVAL DAY TO SECOND.
TO_TIMESTAMP(*string, fmt*)	Converts the character string representation of a date and time to a value of type TIMESTAMP; optionally use format model *fmt*, which defaults to the session NLS_DATE_FORMAT.
TO_TIMESTAMP_TZ(*string, fmt*)	Converts the character string representation of a date and time to a value of type TIMESTAMP WITH TIME ZONE; optionally use format model *fmt*, which defaults to the session NLS_TIMESTAMP_FORMAT.
TO_YMINTERVAL(*string*)	Converts the character string representation of an interval expressed in years and months to a value of INTERVAL YEAR TO MONTH.
TRUNC(*date,fmt*)	Truncates the *date* value to format model *fmt* level of granularity. The default granularity is day.

Built-in function	Description
TZ_OFFSET(*tz*)	Returns the time zone offset from UTC for *tz*, where *tz* is a time zone name, a time zone offset, or the keywords SESSIONTIMEZONE or DBTIMEZONE.

Built-in Regular Expression Functions

The Oracle database supports the use of regular expressions via five built-in functions: REGEXP_COUNT, REGEXP_INSTR, REGEXP_LIKE, REGEXP_REPLACE, and REGEXP_SUBSTR.

Metacharacters

Regular expressions are found in Unix utilities, such as *grep*, *sed*, and the *ex* editor; in the Perl scripting language; and in many other tools. Regular expressions are a powerful and popular means of processing text, mainly because they use *metacharacters* to facilitate searching for strings. The metacharacters supported by the database are shown in the following table:

Pattern metacharacter	Description
*	Asterisk. Matches zero or more occurrences.
+	Plus sign. Matches one or more occurrences.
?	Question mark. Matches zero or one occurrence.
^	Caret. Matches beginning of line.
$	Dollar sign. Matches end of line.
.	Period. Matches any single character.
\	Backslash. Treats the following metacharacter as a nonspecial character.
{*m*}	Curly braces. Matches exactly *m* times.
{*m*,}	Curly braces. Matches at least *m* times.

Pattern metacharacter	Description
{m, n}	Curly braces. Matches at least *m* times, but no more than *n* times.
[]	Square brackets. Matches any of the characters in the square brackets.
|	Vertical bar. Alternation operator for specifying alternative matches.
( )	Parentheses. Grouping expression.
\n	Backslash. Backreference expression (\1 through \9). Used in conjunction with ( ) to identify the *n*th occurrence of the backreferenced expression. (REGEXP_ REPLACE allows up to 500 backreferences in *replacement_string*.)
[: :]	Character class. Examples are [:digit:] for numeric digits or [:alnum:] for alphanumeric characters.
[. .]	Collation element. Encloses multiple characters treated as one character (e.g., 'ch' in Spanish).
[= =]	Equivalence class. Matches accented and unaccented versions of a letter.

REGEXP_COUNT

The REGEXP_COUNT function returns a number containing the tally of the occurences of a regular expression in a specific column, variable, or text literal. The syntax is:

```
REGEXP_COUNT (source_string, pattern [,postion
    [,match_modifier]])
```

where *source_string* is the character string to be searched, *pattern* is the regular expression pattern to search for in the *source_string*, and *match_modifier* is one or more modifiers that apply to the search (see "Match modifiers" on page 104). For example:

```
/* Count #of phone numbers in contact info */
phone_pattern :=
```

```
        '\(?\d{3}\)?[\s.-]?\d{3}[\s-.]?\d{4}';
    phone_count :=
        regep_count (contact_clob, phone_pattern);
```

REGEXP_LIKE

The REGEXP_LIKE function determines whether a specific
column, variable, or text literal contains text matching a regular
expression. It returns Boolean TRUE if the regular expression
is found in the *source_string* and FALSE if the regular expression is not found. The syntax is:

```
REGEXP_LIKE (source_string, pattern [,match_modi
fier])
```

where *source_string* is the character string to be searched, *pattern* is the regular expression pattern to search for in
source_string, and *match_modifier* is one or more modifiers
that apply to the search. For example:

```
IF REGEXP_LIKE(phone_number,'^\(?212\)?'
THEN
    -- phone number begins with 212
    -- optionally enclosed by parentheses
    apply_nyc_surcharge;
END IF;
```

REGEXP_INSTR

The REGEXP_INSTR function locates, by character position,
an occurrence of text matching a regular expression pattern. It
returns the beginning or ending position of the regular expression within a string. The syntax is:

```
REGEXP_INSTR (source_string, pattern
[,beginning_position [,occurrence [,return_option
[,match_modifier [,subexp]]]]])
```

where *source_string* is a character string to be searched, *pattern*
is a regular expression pattern to search for in *source_string*,
beginning_position is the character position at which to begin
the search, *occurrence* is the ordinal occurrence desired (1 =

first, 2 = second, etc.), *return_option* is either 0 for the beginning position or 1 for the ending position, and *match_modifier* is one or more modifiers that apply to the search. You can also specify *subexp*; if the pattern uses subexpressions, this parameter tells the database which subexpression to return the position of from the pattern found in the source string. Subexpressions are used to parse out the interesting pieces. You define a subexpression by enclosing it in parentheses. For example:

```
witty_saying :=
    'Man fears time, but time fears the Pyramids';
-- Display the witty_saying
-- starting w/ 2nd occurence of the word 'time'
DBMS_OUTPUT.PUT_LINE(
    SUBSTR(witty_saying
        ,REGEXP_INSTR(witty_saying,'time',1,2)));
```

The output is:

```
time fears the Pyramids
```

REGEXP_SUBSTR

The REGEXP_SUBSTR function extracts text matching a regular expression from a character column, variable, or text literal. It returns as many matching substrings as it finds (which might be zero). The syntax is:

```
REGEXP_SUBSTR (source_string, pattern [,position
[,occurrence [,match_modifier [,subexp]]]])
```

where *source_string* is the character string to be searched, *pattern* is the regular expression pattern to search for in *source_string*, *position* is the character position at which to begin the search, *occurrence* is the ordinal occurrence desired (1 = first, 2 = second, etc.), and *match_modifier* is one or more modifiers that apply to the search. You can also specify *subexp*; if the pattern uses subexpressions, this parameter tells the database which subexpression to return from the pattern found in the source string. For example:

```
-- get the leading number part of the address
-- (up to a whitespace character)
street_num := REGEXP_SUBSTR (
    address_line1,'[[:digit:]]+[:space:]');
```

In the following example, we parse out the exchange (second group of three digits) from the first telephone number found in the variable c_rec.c_clob. The regular expression pattern is defined as three digits optionally enclosed by parentheses; followed by an optional dot, dash, or whitespace character; followed by three digits; followed by an optional dot, dash, or whitespace character; followed by four digits. The whole pattern must match for the substring to be recognized as a matching pattern (telephone number). We then parse out the interesting part—the middle three digits—and assign it to the variable exchange. Here is the example data:

```
SELECT * FROM contacts WHERE contact_id=26;

CONTACT_ID CONTACT_NAME        CONTACT_CLOB
---------- ------------        ------------
26 Elwood Blues                Brother of
                               "Joliet" Jake
                               address:
                               1060 W Addison St
                               Chicago, IL 60613
                               home 773-555-5253
                               club 312-555-2468
```

Next is the subexpression parsing example:

```
DECLARE
  ptrn     VARCHAR2(45);
  exchange VARCHAR2(3);
  CURSOR c_cur IS
    SELECT contact_clob c_clob
    FROM contacts WHERE contact_id=26;
BEGIN
  ptrn :=
  '\(?(\d{3})\)?[\s.-]?(\d{3})[\s.-]?(\d{4})';
  -- Get the second subexpression from the first
```

```
   -- occurrence of the pattern
   FOR c_rec in c_cur LOOP
      exchange :=
        REGEXP_SUBSTR(c_rec.c_clob,ptrn,1,1,'i',2);
      DBMS_OUTPUT.PUT_LINE(
        'exchange='||exchange);
   END LOOP;
END;
```

This displays:

```
exchange=555
```

REGEXP_REPLACE

The REGEXP_REPLACE function replaces a regular expression with new text that you specify. Your replacement text may include back references to values in the regular expression. The syntax is:

```
REGEXP_REPLACE (source_string, pattern
[,replacement_string [,position [,occurrence
[,match_modifier]]]])
```

where *source_string* is the character string to be searched, *pattern* is the regular expression pattern to search for in *source_string*, *replacement_string* is the replacement text for *pattern*, *position* is the character position at which to begin the search, *occurrence* is the ordinal occurrence desired (0 = all occurrences, 1 = first, 2 = second, etc.), and *match_modifier* is one or more modifiers that apply to the search. For example:

```
-- Change the domain part of the email addresses
-- Replace all between the @ and the '.com' with
-- the new domain name
REGEXP_REPLACE(email_address
             , '@.*\.com', '@new_domain.com'));
```

Match modifiers

The *match_modifiers* available to the regular expression condition and functions are shown in the following table:

---

match_modifier	Description
i	Uses a case-insensitive search; the default behavior is based on NLS_SORT.
c	Uses a case-sensitive search; the default behavior is based on NLS_SORT.
n	Enables the dot metacharacter to match newlines.
m	Treats the *source_string* as multiple lines for purposes of the beginning and end-of-line metacharacters ^ and $.

For more details, see the *Oracle Regular Expressions Pocket Reference*, by Jonathan Gennick and Peter Linsley (O'Reilly).

Stored Procedures and Functions

PL/SQL allows you to create a variety of named program units, or containers, for your code. These include:

Procedure
   A program that executes one or more statements.

Function
   A program that executes one or more statements and returns a value.

Trigger
   A program that executes in response to database changes.

Package
   A container for procedures, functions, and data structures.

Object type
   Oracle's version of an object-oriented class; object types can contain member procedures and functions.

The following sections describe stored procedures and functions. Later sections describe triggers, packages, and object types.

Procedures

Procedures are program units that execute one or more statements and can receive or return zero or more values through their parameter lists. The syntax of a procedure is:

```
CREATE [OR REPLACE] PROCEDURE name
    [ (parameter[,parameter]) ]
    [AUTHID { CURRENT_USER | DEFINER } ]
    [ACCESSIBLE BY (program_unit_list)]
{ IS | AS }
    declaration_section
BEGIN
    executable_section
[EXCEPTION
    exception_section]
END [name];
```

where ACCESSIBLE BY is only available for 12.1 and higher.

Inside a PL/SQL executable section, a procedure is called as a standalone executable statement:

```
apply_discount(new_company_id, 0.15);
```

Many execution environments, such as SQL*Plus, also support ANSI SQL's CALL syntax:

```
CALL apply_discount(new_company_id, 0.15);
```

However, SQL*Plus programmers commonly invoke procedures with the SQL*Plus EXEC command (short for EXECUTE):

```
EXEC apply_discount(new_company_id, 0.15);
```

or the equivalent anonymous block:

```
BEGIN
    apply_discount(new_company_id, 0.15);
END;
```

Functions

Functions are program units that execute zero or more statements and return a value through the RETURN clause. Functions also can receive or return zero or more values through their parameter lists. The syntax of a function is:

```
CREATE [OR REPLACE] FUNCTION name
     [ (parameter [,parameter]) ]
   RETURN return_datatype
   [AUTHID { CURRENT_USER | DEFINER } ]
   [DETERMINISTIC]
   [PARALLEL_ENABLE [partition_clause]]
   [PIPELINED [USING implementation_type]]
   [RESULT_CACHE]
   [ACCESSIBLE BY (program_unit_list)]
   [AGGREGATE USING implementation_type]
{ IS | AS }
   [declaration_section]
BEGIN
   executable_section
[EXCEPTION
   exception_section]
END [name];
```

where ACCESSIBLE BY is only available for 12.1 and higher.

A function must have at least one RETURN statement in the execution section. The RETURN clause in the function header specifies the datatype of the returned value.

See "Compiling Stored PL/SQL Programs" on page 152 for information on the keywords OR REPLACE, AUTHID, DETERMINISTIC, PARALLEL_ENABLE, PIPELINED, and AGGREGATE USING. See "Privileges and Stored PL/SQL" on page 118 for AUTHID. See "Function Result Cache" on page 116 for RESULT_CACHE.

A function can be called anywhere that an expression of the same type can be used. You can call a function:

- In an assignment statement:

```
sales07 := tot_sales(2007,'C');
```

- To set a default value:

```
DECLARE
   sales07 NUMBER DEFAULT tot_sales(2007,'C');
BEGIN
```

- In a Boolean expression:

```
IF tot_sales(2007,'C') > 10000
THEN ...
```

- In a SQL statement (note that there are special rules that apply to calling a user-defined function inside SQL; see "Calling PL/SQL Functions in SQL" on page 134):

```
SELECT first_name, surname
   FROM sellers
WHERE tot_sales(2007,'C') > 1000;
```

- As an argument in another program unit's parameter list

Here, for example, max_discount is a programmer-defined function, and SYSDATE is a built-in function:

```
apply_discount(company_id, max_discount(SYSDATE));
```

Parameters

Procedures, functions, and cursors may have a parameter list. This list contains one or more parameters that allow you to pass information back and forth between the subprogram and the calling program. Each parameter is defined by its name, datatype, mode, and optional default value. The syntax for a parameter is:

```
parameter_name [mode] [NOCOPY] datatype[ { := |
DEFAULT } value]
```

Datatype

The datatype can be any PL/SQL or programmer-defined data-type but cannot be constrained by a size (NUMBER is valid, NUMBER(10) is not valid). The actual size of the parameter is determined from the calling program:

```
CREATE OR REPLACE PROCEDURE empid_to_name
   (in_id           emp.emp_id%TYPE -- Compiles OK
   ,last_name  VARCHAR2         -- Compiles OK
   ,first_name VARCHAR2(10)     -- Won't compile
   )
```

The lengths of out_last_name and out_first_name are deter-mined by the calling program:

```
DECLARE
   surname      VARCHAR2(10);
   first_name   VARCHAR2(10);
BEGIN
   empid_to_name(10, surname, first_name);
END;
```

Mode

The *mode* of a parameter specifies whether the parameter can be read from or written to, as shown in the following table:

Mode	Description	Parameter usage
IN	Read-only	The value of the actual parameter can be referenced inside the program, but the parameter cannot be changed.
IN OUT	Read/write	The program can both reference (read) and modify (write) the parameter.
OUT	Write	The value of any argument passed in is ignored; thereafter, the program can modify the parameter and read its value, passing the final value out.

If the mode is not explicitly defined, it defaults to IN.

OUT parameters are not the same as IN OUT parameters. When running the called program, the runtime engine ignores (sets to NULL) any argument value you supply for an OUT parameter; it preserves the value provided for an IN OUT. If an exception is raised during execution of a procedure or function, assignments made to OUT or IN OUT parameters get rolled back unless the parameter includes the NOCOPY option.

NOCOPY is a request to the compiler to make the parameter a call by reference instead of a call by value. Normally, PL/SQL passes IN/OUT parameters by value—a copy of the parameter is created for the subprogram. When parameter items are large (as may be the case with CLOBs, objects, and collections), the copy can eat memory and slow down processing. NOCOPY asks PL/SQL to pass the parameter by reference, using a pointer to the single copy of the parameter.

The main disadvantage of NOCOPY is that when an exception is raised during execution of a program that has modified an OUT or IN OUT parameter, the changes to the actual parameters are not "rolled back" because the parameters were passed by reference instead of being copied. Also, NOCOPY does not always apply; see *Oracle PL/SQL Programming* for a list of cases in which the compiler ignores the NOCOPY request.

Default values

IN parameters can be given default values (usually either the DEFAULT keyword or the := operator). If an IN parameter has a default value, you do not need to supply an argument for that parameter when you call the program unit. It automatically uses the default value. For example:

```
CREATE OR REPLACE PROCEDURE hire_employee
    (emp_id        IN VARCHAR2
    ,hire_date     IN DATE := SYSDATE
    ,company_id    IN NUMBER DEFAULT 1
    )
IS
    ...
```

Here are some example calls to the preceding procedure:

```
-- Use two default values.
hire_employee(new_empno);
-- Use one default value.
hire_employee(new_empno,'12-Jan-2007');
-- Use nontrailing default value, named notation.
hire_employee(emp_id => new_empno, company_id =>
12);
```

Parameter-passing notations

Formal parameters are the names that are declared in the header of a procedure or function. *Actual parameters (arguments)* are the values or expressions placed in the parameter list when a procedure or function is called. In the empid_to_name example shown earlier in "Datatype" on page 109, the formal parameters to the procedure are in_id, out_last_name, and out_first_name. The actual parameters used in the call to this procedure are 10, surname, and first_name.

PL/SQL lets you use either of two styles for passing arguments in parameter lists:

Positional notation
> The default. Each value in the list of arguments supplied in the program call is associated with the parameter in the corresponding position.

Named notation
> Explicitly associates the argument value with its parameter by name (not position). When you use named notation, you can supply the arguments in any order, and you can omit IN arguments that have default values.

The call to the empid_to_name procedure is shown here with both notations:

```
BEGIN
   -- Implicit positional notation.
   empid_to_name(10, surname, first_name);

   -- Explicit named notation.
   empid_to_name(in_id => 10
      ,out_last_name => surname
      ,out_first_name => first_name);
END;
```

You may combine positional and named notation, as long as positional arguments appear to the left of any named notation arguments; for example:

```
empid_to_name (
   10, surname
 , out_first_name => first_name);
```

As of Oracle Database 11g, you can use both positional and named notation when calling stored functions inside a SQL statement.

Local Programs

A local program is a procedure or function that is defined in the declaration section of a PL/SQL block. The declaration of a local program must appear at the end of the declaration section, after the declarations of any types, records, cursors, variables, and exceptions. A program defined in a declaration section may be referenced only within that block's execution and exception sections. It is not defined outside that block.

The following program defines a local procedure and function:

```
PROCEDURE track_revenue
IS
   l_total NUMBER;

   PROCEDURE calc_total (year_in IN INTEGER) IS
   BEGIN
      calculations here ...
   END;
```

```
   FUNCTION below_minimum (comp_id IN INTEGER)
      RETURN BOOLEAN
   IS
   BEGIN
      ...
   END;
BEGIN
   ...main procedure logic here
END;
```

Local programs may be overloaded with the same restrictions as overloaded packaged programs.

Program Overloading

PL/SQL allows you to define two or more programs with the same name within any declaration section, when declared in a package specification or body. This is called *overloading*. If two or more programs have the same name, they must be different in some other way so that the compiler can determine which program should be used.

Here is an example of overloaded programs in a built-in package specification:

```
PACKAGE DBMS_OUTPUT
IS
   PROCEDURE PUT_LINE (a VARCHAR2);
   PROCEDURE PUT_LINE (a NUMBER);
   PROCEDURE PUT_LINE (a DATE);
END;
```

Each PUT_LINE procedure is identical, except for the datatype of the parameter. That is enough difference for the compiler.

To overload programs successfully, one or more of the following conditions must be true:

- Parameters must differ by datatype family (number, character, datetime, or Boolean).

- The program type must be different (you can overload a function and a procedure of the same name and identical parameter list).

- The numbers of parameters must be different.

In general, you *cannot* overload programs if:

- Only the datatypes of the functions' RETURN clauses are different.

- Parameter datatypes are within the same family (CHAR and VARCHAR2, NUMBER and INTEGER, etc.).

- Only the modes of the parameters are different (IN versus IN OUT, for example).

- The programs are standalone functions or procedures.

You can overload programs whose parameters differ only in numeric datatypes, as long as they are in different datatype "families." The runtime environment will search first for a matching program with a PLS_INTEGER (or the equivalent BINARY_INTEGER) parameter; then it will try to match NUMBER, then, BINARY_FLOAT, and finally BINARY_DOUBLE, in that order. If you want to force the use of the faster IEEE 754 datatypes, you may need to use the TO_BINARY_FLOAT or TO_BINARY_DOUBLE functions on the input argument, or for literals, append with f or d, as discussed in "Numeric Literals" on page 5.

Forward Declarations

Programs must be declared before they can be used. PL/SQL supports *mutual recursion*, in which program A calls program B, whereupon program B calls program A. To implement this mutual recursion, you must use a *forward declaration* of the programs. This technique declares a program in advance of the program definition, thus making it available for other programs to use. The forward declaration is the program header up to the IS/AS keyword:

```
PROCEDURE perform_calc(year_in IN NUMBER)
IS
   /* Forward decl for total_cost function. */
   FUNCTION total_cost (year_in IN NUMBER)
      RETURN NUMBER;
   /* net_profit function can use total_cost. */
   FUNCTION net_profit(year_in IN NUMBER)
      RETURN NUMBER
   IS
   BEGIN
      RETURN total_sales(year_in) -
             total_cost(year_in);
   END;

   /* Implementation of total_cost function */
   FUNCTION total_cost (year_in IN NUMBER)
      RETURN NUMBER
   IS
   BEGIN
      IF net_profit(year_in) < 0 THEN
         RETURN 0;
      ELSE
         RETURN...;
      END IF;
   END;
BEGIN
   ...
END perform_calc;
```

Table Functions

Table functions are functions that can be called within the
FROM clause of a query, as if they were relational tables. To act
as a table function, a function must have a header that is SQL-
compatible (no Boolean arguments, for example), and the
function must return a supported collection type: either a nested table or VARRAY whose type is declared at the schema
level. As of Oracle Database 12c, a SQL statement embedded in
PL/SQL *can* use a table function typed as an associative array
that you have declared in a package spec.

Pipelined table functions are special cases of table functions that allow you to "pipe" data out of the function back to the calling query while the function is still executing. Here is a very simple example of a pipelined table function:

```
CREATE TYPE num_tab_typ AS TABLE OF NUMBER;
/

CREATE OR REPLACE FUNCTION piped_func(
      factor IN NUMBER)
   RETURN num_tab_typ PIPELINED AS
BEGIN
   FOR counter IN 1..1000
   LOOP
     PIPE ROW (counter*factor);
   END LOOP;
   RETURN;
END piped_func;
/

SELECT COLUMN_VALUE FROM TABLE (piped_func (2))
 WHERE rownum < 5;

COLUMN_VALUE
------------
            2
            4
            6
            8
```

Function Result Cache

With the PL/SQL function result cache, you can tell the database to retain the results of your function in a cache, located in the System Global Area (SGA), and available to all sessions that invoke the function. The RESULT_CACHE feature is best suited for functions that are executed relatively often (think every few seconds or minutes) against data that changes relatively slowly (think hourly or daily). Oracle will automatically ensure that the function results are flushed whenever there is

DML on any table or view used by the function. In a RAC environment, each instance has its own result cache, which may differ in which items are cached, but common items in different instances will never disagree with each other.

Whenever a result-cached function is called with new parameters, both the parameters and the return value are saved in the cache. When the result-cached function is called with cached parameters, whether from your session or from a different one, the results are returned from the cache instead of being calculated anew. These cached entries can be monitored with the V$RESULT_CACHE% series of data dictionary views. Tune the size and usage of the result cache with the RESULT_CACHE_SIZE and RESULT_CACHE_MODE initialization parameters and the DBMS_RESULT_CACHE built-in package.

To enable result caching for your function, it must *not* be:

- In an anonymous block
- Defined with invoker's rights
- A pipelined table function
- Defined with any OUT or IN OUT parameters
- Defined with any IN parameters of type BLOB, CLOB, NCLOB, REF CURSOR, object, or record
- Defined with a RETURN type of BLOB, CLOB, NCLOB, REF CURSOR, object, or compound datatype (record or collection) containing any of these unsupported types
- Dependent on session-specific settings or application contexts

Oracle recommends that result-cached functions not modify the database state or external state. For example, result-cached functions should not call DBMS_OUTPUT or UTL_FILE or send email because these external operations will not execute consistently between result cache hits and misses. Recursive fuctions are good candidates for result caching. The factorial function is an example:

```
CREATE OR REPLACE FUNCTION factorial(n NUMBER)
RETURN NUMBER RESULT_CACHE IS
BEGIN
  IF n <= 1 THEN
    RETURN 1;
  ELSE
    RETURN n*factorial(n-1);
  END IF;
END;
```

For packaged functions, use the keyword RESULT_CACHE in both the package specification and the package body:

```
CREATE OR REPLACE PACKAGE bi_sales IS
  FUNCTION avg_sales(cust_id IN NUMBER)
    RETURN NUMBER RESULT_CACHE;
END bi_sales;

CREATE OR REPLACE PACKAGE BODY bi_sales IS
  FUNCTION avg_sales(cust_id IN NUMBER)
    RETURN NUMBER RESULT_CACHE IS
  BEGIN
    ...
  END;
END bi_sales;
```

Privileges and Stored PL/SQL

An Oracle user who creates a stored program will be able to execute that program unless nondefault privileges are in place. For other Oracle users to run the program, they would, at a minimum, need to be granted EXECUTE permission on it. This permission can be received via direct grant to the user, or via a grant to a database role that has been granted to the user.

When a user executes a stored procedure, Oracle has to evaluate whether the user has permissions on the underlying objects (tables, views, procedures, etc.) that the procedure uses internally. To make this decision, Oracle supports two different models for evaluating names and privileges at runtime.

The default model is *definer rights*, which executes the stored program with the privileges of the *owner* of the program. This model works well in most cases. If the program refers to objects that the program owner does not also own, the grants on those must be directly to him—he cannot inherit these privileges from a role.

The other model, known as *invoker rights*, causes Oracle to resolve program identifiers and execute the program, with the permissions of the user who is *running* the program. Stored programs that include the keywords AUTHID CURRENT_USER will run with invoker rights; anonymous PL/SQL blocks always execute with invoker rights.

Be aware that Oracle performs additional runtime checks, and incurs a slight performance overhead, when running an invoker rights program that uses any database objects.

By default, an invoker rights program can use the full range of the invoker's database permissions at runtime, even if those privileges exceed the programmer's. In other words, an invoker rights program "inherits" the privileges of the invoker, and a programmer could (either intentionally or accidentally) write code that would perform an operation beyond his or her pay grade.

To help guard against such misuse, Oracle Database 12*c* introduced the INHERIT [ANY] PRIVILEGES feature. An end user or DBA could prevent such inheritance at the user level by issuing the following REVOKE statement:

```
REVOKE INHERIT PRIVILEGE ON invoking_user FROM
PUBLIC;
```

or:

```
REVOKE INHERIT PRIVILEGE ON invoking_user FROM
unit_owner;
```

Any subsequent privilege escalation attempt by an invoker rights program that is run by *invoking_user* will result in a runtime failure ORA-06598: insufficient INHERIT PRIVILEGES privilege. Significantly, this failure cannot be trapped as an exception in the program.

For backward compatibility, Oracle automatically runs GRANT INHERIT PRIVILEGE ON username TO PUBLIC when a database user is migrated or created.

Even with EXECUTE privilege and an appropriate runtime rights model, there is another mechanism that may limit one program's ability to invoke another: the ACCESSIBLE BY feature. Using this clause in a program specification restricts which programs can invoke it to those explicitly listed in the clause. This is a program-level, rather than a user-level, restriction, so it applies even when the same user owns both the called program and its calling program.

Triggers

Triggers are programs that execute in response to changes in table data or certain database events. A predefined set of events can be "hooked" with a trigger, enabling you to integrate your own processing with that of the database. A triggering event *fires* or executes the trigger.

There are three types of triggering events:

DML events
> Fire when an INSERT, UPDATE, or DELETE statement executes

DDL events
> Fire when a CREATE, ALTER, or DROP statement executes

Database events
> Fire when one of the predefined database-level events occurs

Complete lists of these events are included in later sections.

Creating Triggers

The syntax for creating a trigger on a DML event is:

```
CREATE [OR REPLACE] TRIGGER trigger_name
{ BEFORE | AFTER | INSTEAD OF | FOR } trigger_event
   ON {table_or_view_reference |
      NESTED TABLE nested_table_column OF view}
      [REFERENCING [OLD AS old] [NEW AS new]
         [PARENT AS parent]]
[FOR EACH ROW ]
[FOLLOWS other_trigger] [DISABLE]
[COMPOUND TRIGGER]
[WHEN trigger_condition]
trigger_body;
```

The syntax for creating a trigger on a DDL or database event is:

```
CREATE [OR REPLACE] TRIGGER trigger_name
{ BEFORE | AFTER } trigger_event
   ON [ DATABASE | schema ]
 [FOLLOWS other_trigger][DISABLE]
[WHEN trigger_condition]
trigger_body;
```

Trigger events are listed in the following table:

Trigger event	Description
INSERT	Fires whenever a row is added to the table_or_view_reference.
UPDATE	Fires whenever an UPDATE changes the table_or_view_reference. UPDATE triggers can additionally specify an OF clause to restrict firing to updates of certain columns.
DELETE	Fires whenever a row is deleted from the table_or_view_reference. Does not fire on a TRUNCATE of the table.

Trigger event	Description
ALTER	Fires whenever an ALTER statement changes a database object. In this context, objects are things such as tables or packages (found in ALL_OBJECTS). Can apply to a single schema or the entire database.
ANALYZE	Fires whenever the database collects or deletes statistics or validates the structure of a database object.
ASSOCIATE STATISTICS	Fires whenever the database associates a statistic type with a database object.
AUDIT	Fires whenever the database records an audit operation.
COMMENT	Fires whenever a comment on a database object is modified.
CREATE	Fires whenever a database object is created. Does not fire on CREATE CONTROLFILE statements.
DB_ROLE_CHANGE	In a Data Guard configuration, fires whenever a role change from primary to standby or standby to primary occurs. Only AFTER DB_ROLE_CHANGE triggers on the DATABASE are allowed.
DDL	Fires whenever one of the following events occurs: ALTER, ANALYZE, ASSOCIATE STATISTICS, AUDIT, COMMENT, CREATE, DISASSOCIATE, DROP, GRANT, NOAUDIT, RENAME, REVOKE, or TRUNCATE.
DISASSOCIATE STATISTICS	Fires whenever the database disassociates a statistic type from a database object.
DROP	Fires whenever a DROP statement removes an object from the database. In this context, objects are things such as tables or packages (found in ALL_OBJECTS). Can apply to a single schema or the entire database.
GRANT	Fires whenever a system, role, or object privilege is assigned.
NOAUDIT	Fires whenever the database processes a NOAUDIT statement to stop auditing database operations.

Trigger event	Description
RENAME	Fires whenever a RENAME statement changes a database object name.
REVOKE	Fires whenever a system, role, or object privilege is rescinded.
TRUNCATE	Fires whenever a TRUNCATE statement is processed to purge a table or cluster.
SERVERERROR	Fires whenever a server error message is logged. Only AFTER triggers are allowed in this context.
LOGON	Fires whenever a session is created (a user connects to the database). Only AFTER triggers are allowed in this context.
LOGOFF	Fires whenever a session is terminated (a user disconnects from the database). Only BEFORE triggers are allowed in this context.
STARTUP	Fires when the database is opened. Only AFTER triggers are allowed in this context.
SHUTDOWN	Fires when the database is closed. Only BEFORE triggers are allowed in this context.
SUSPEND	Fires whenever a server error causes a transaction to be suspended.

Triggers can fire BEFORE or AFTER the triggering event. AFTER DML triggers are slightly more efficient than BEFORE triggers.

The REFERENCING clause is allowed only for the data events INSERT, UPDATE, and DELETE. It lets you give a nondefault name to the old and new pseudorecords. These pseudo-records give the program visibility to the pre- and postchange values in row-level triggers. These records are defined like %ROWTYPE records, except that columns of type LONG or LONG RAW cannot be referenced. They are prefixed with a colon in the trigger body and referenced with dot notation. Unlike other records, these fields can only be assigned individually—aggregate assignment is not allowed. All old fields are NULL within

INSERT triggers, and all new fields are NULL within DELETE triggers. Parent fields are valid only in triggers on nested tables and refer to the current row in the parent table.

FOR EACH ROW defines the trigger to be a row-level trigger. Row-level triggers fire once for each row affected. The default is a statement-level trigger, which fires only once for each triggering statement.

If you have multiple triggers on the same event, you can use the FOLLOWS keyword to define the order in which they fire.

If you specify the DISABLE keyword, the database creates the trigger in a disabled state. You can then issue ALTER TRIGGER ENABLE or ALTER TABLE ENABLE ALL TRIGGERS to enable the trigger. Creating a trigger in a disabled state allows you to verify that it will compile and helps you avoid "ORA-04098: trigger NAME is invalid and failed re-validation" errors.

The WHEN *trigger_condition* specifies the conditions that must be met for the trigger to fire. Stored functions and object methods are not allowed in the trigger condition.

The trigger body is a standard PL/SQL block. For example:

```
CREATE OR REPLACE TRIGGER add_tstamp
   BEFORE INSERT ON emp
   REFERENCING NEW as new_row
   FOR EACH ROW
   FOLLOWS audit_emp
   BEGIN
      -- Automatically timestamp the entry.
      SELECT CURRENT_TIMESTAMP
        INTO :new_row.entry_timestamp
        FROM dual;
END add_tstamp;
```

Triggers are enabled by default on creation and can be disabled (so that they do not fire) with an ALTER statement, issued with the following syntax:

```
ALTER TRIGGER trigger_name { ENABLE | DISABLE };

ALTER TABLE table_name { ENABLE | DISABLE } ALL
TRIGGERS;
```

Trigger Predicates

When using a single trigger for multiple events, use the trigger
predicates INSERTING, UPDATING, and DELETING in the
trigger condition to identify the triggering event, as shown in
this example:

```
CREATE OR REPLACE TRIGGER emp_log_t
   AFTER INSERT OR UPDATE OR DELETE ON emp
   FOR EACH ROW
DECLARE
   dmltype  CHAR(1);
BEGIN
   IF INSERTING THEN
       dmltype := 'I';
       INSERT INTO emp_log (emp_no, who, operation)
          VALUES (:new.empno, USER, dmltype);
   ELSIF UPDATING  THEN
       dmltype := 'U';
       INSERT INTO emp_log (emp_no, who, operation)
          VALUES (:new.empno, USER, dmltype);
   END IF;
END;
```

DML Events

The DML events include INSERT, UPDATE, and DELETE
statements on a table. An INSTEAD OF trigger is associated
with a view and fires in lieu of DML to that view. Triggers on
these events can be statement-level triggers (table only) or row-
level triggers, and can fire BEFORE or AFTER the triggering
event. BEFORE triggers can modify the data in affected rows,
but perform an additional logical read. AFTER triggers do not
perform this additional logical read and therefore perform
slightly better, but are not able to change the :new values.

AFTER triggers are thus better suited for data-validation functionality. Triggers cannot be created on SYS-owned objects. The order in which these triggers fire, if present, is as follows:

1. BEFORE statement-level trigger
2. BEFORE row-level trigger for each row affected by statement
3. The triggering statement
4. AFTER row-level trigger for each row affected by statement
5. AFTER statement-level trigger

Compound DML Triggers

Compound triggers allow you to combine up to four DML triggering events into a single coordinated program. These compound triggers let you share common elements (subprograms and state data) among the different triggering events; for example, you can use bulk binds in your DML trigger and achieve significantly better performance when several rows are affected by a statement.

A compound trigger has as many as four sections: a BEFORE STATEMENT section, a BEFORE EACH ROW section, an AFTER EACH ROW section, and an AFTER STATEMENT section. The FOR and COMPOUND TRIGGER keywords tell the database that the trigger is a compound trigger. In the compound trigger's declaration section, you declare the structures that are to be shared by all sections. These structures include the collections needed for bulk binds, variables, local programs, etc. This trigger data is created when the trigger fires and is automatically destroyed (cleaned up) when the triggering statement completes.

Here is an example of using a compound trigger to record audit information on changes to the salary column in the employee table. The example shows how this is done with the old FOR

EACH ROW technique as well as the newer, more efficient bulk binds:

```
-- First row-by-row way
CREATE OR REPLACE TRIGGER old_trg
  AFTER UPDATE OF salary ON employees
  FOR EACH ROW
BEGIN
  INSERT INTO employee_audit
    VALUES (:new.employee_id
           ,:old.salary
           ,:new.salary ,SYSTIMESTAMP);
END old_trg;

/* This next trigger is created disabled and
   must be enabled for use
   Here is the bulk bind approach: */
CREATE OR REPLACE TRIGGER new_trg
  FOR UPDATE OF salary ON employees DISABLE
  COMPOUND TRIGGER
    -- General declarations here
    TYPE emp_aud_t IS TABLE OF
        employee_audit%ROWTYPE
        INDEX BY BINARY_INTEGER;
    emps emp_aud_t;
    cntr  PLS_INTEGER := 0;
    batch_size CONSTANT PLS_INTEGER := 100;

    -- local procedure
    PROCEDURE bulk_flush IS
    BEGIN
      FORALL idx IN 1..emps.count
        INSERT INTO employee_audit
            VALUES emps(idx);
      emps.delete;
      cntr := 0;
    END ;

    -- Each section is defined like this:
    AFTER EACH ROW IS
    BEGIN
```

```
   cntr := cntr+1;
   emps(cntr).employee_id := :new.employee_id;
   emps(cntr).old_salary := :old.salary;
   emps(cntr).new_salary := :new.salary;
   emps(cntr).change_ts := systimestamp;
   IF cntr >= batch_size THEN
      bulk_flush;
   END IF;
END AFTER EACH ROW;

-- Final flush in after statement section
AFTER STATEMENT IS
BEGIN
   bulk_flush;
END AFTER STATEMENT;
END new_trg;
```

DDL Events

The DDL events are ALTER, ANALYZE, ASSOCIATE STA-
TISTICS, AUDIT, COMMENT, CREATE, DISASSOCIATE,
DROP, GRANT, NOAUDIT, RENAME, REVOKE, and TRUN-
CATE. These triggers fire whenever the respective DDL state-
ment is executed. DDL triggers can apply to either a single
schema or the entire database.

Database Events

The database events are SERVERERROR, LOGON, LOGOFF,
STARTUP, SHUTDOWN, and SUSPEND. Only BEFORE trig-
gers are allowed for LOGOFF and SHUTDOWN events. Only
AFTER triggers are allowed for LOGON, STARTUP, and
SERVERERROR events. A SHUTDOWN trigger will fire on a
SHUTDOWN NORMAL and a SHUTDOWN IMMEDIATE,
but not on a SHUTDOWN ABORT.

Packages

A package is a collection of PL/SQL elements that are grouped together. There are several benefits to using packages, including information hiding, object-oriented design, top-down design, object persistence across transactions, and improved performance.

Elements that can be placed in a package include procedures, functions, constants, variables, cursors, exception names, and TYPE statements (for associative arrays, records, REF CURSORs, etc.).

Package Structure

A package can have two parts: the specification and the body. The *package specification* is required and lists all the objects that are "publicly" available (i.e., may be referenced from outside the package) for use in applications. It also provides all the information a developer needs to use objects in the package; essentially, it is the package's API.

The *package body* contains all the code needed to implement procedures, functions, and cursors listed in the specification, as well as any private objects (accessible only to other elements defined in that package) and an optional initialization section.

If a package specification does not contain any procedures or functions, and no private code is needed, that package does not need to have a package body.

The syntax for the package specification is:

```
CREATE [OR REPLACE] PACKAGE package_name
   [AUTHID { CURRENT_USER | DEFINER } ]
   [ACCESSIBLE BY (program_unit_list)]
{ IS | AS }
   [definitions of public TYPEs
   ,declarations of public variables, types, and
objects
   ,declarations of exceptions
```

```
    ,pragmas
    ,declarations of cursors, procedures, and
  functions
    ,headers of procedures and functions]
END [package_name];
```

The syntax for the package body is:

```
CREATE [OR REPLACE] PACKAGE BODY package_name
    { IS | AS }
    [definitions of private TYPEs
    ,declarations of private variables, types, and
  objects
    ,full definitions of cursors
    ,full definitions of procedures and functions]
[BEGIN
    executable_statements
[EXCEPTION
    exception_handlers]]
END [package_name];
```

Specify the optional OR REPLACE to rebuild an existing package, preserving any EXECUTE privileges previously granted to other accounts. The declarations in the specifications cannot be repeated in the body. Both the execution section and the exception section are optional in a package body. If the execution section is present, it is called the *initialization section* and executes only once—the first time any package element is referenced during a session.

You must compile the package specification before the body specification. When you grant EXECUTE authority on a package to another schema or to PUBLIC, you are giving access only to the specification; the body remains hidden.

Here's an example of a package:

```
CREATE OR REPLACE PACKAGE time_pkg
AS
    FUNCTION GetTimestamp RETURN DATE;
    PROCEDURE ResetTimestamp(
        new_time DATE DEFAULT SYSDATE);
```

```
   END time_pkg;

    -- StartTimeStamp is package-level data.
CREATE OR REPLACE PACKAGE BODY time_pkg
AS

   StartTimeStamp DATE := SYSDATE;

   FUNCTION GetTimestamp RETURN DATE IS
   BEGIN
      RETURN StartTimeStamp;
   END GetTimestamp;

   PROCEDURE ResetTimestamp(
      new_time DATE DEFAULT SYSDATE)
   IS
   BEGIN
      StartTimeStamp := new_time;
   END ResetTimestamp;

   END time_pkg;
```

Referencing Package Elements

The elements declared in the specification are referenced from
the calling application via dot notation:

package_name.package_element

For example, the built-in package DBMS_OUTPUT has a procedure PUT_LINE, so a call to this package would look like
this:

```
DBMS_OUTPUT.PUT_LINE('This is parameter data');
```

Package Data

Data structures declared within a package specification or
body, but outside any procedure or function in the package, are
package data. The default lifetime of package data is your entire

session, spanning transaction boundaries and acting as globals for your programs.

Keep the following guidelines in mind as you work with package data:

- The state of your package variables is not affected by COMMITs and ROLLBACKs.

- A cursor declared in a package has global scope. It remains OPEN until you close it explicitly or until your session ends.

- A good practice is to *hide* your data structures in the package body and provide "get and set" programs to read and write that data. This technique can help protect your data.

SERIALLY_REUSABLE Pragma

If you need package data to exist only during a call to the packaged functions or procedures and not between calls of the current session, you can potentially save runtime memory by using the pragma SERIALLY_REUSABLE. After each call, PL/SQL closes the cursors and releases the memory used in the package. This technique is applicable only to large user communities executing the same routine. Normally, the database server's memory requirements grow linearly with the number of users; with SERIALLY_REUSABLE, this growth can be less than linear because work areas for package states are kept in a pool in the database's SGA and are shared among all users. This pragma must appear in both the specification and the body, as shown here:

```
CREATE OR REPLACE PACKAGE my_pkg IS
   PRAGMA SERIALLY_REUSABLE;
   PROCEDURE gig_em;
END my_pkg;

CREATE OR REPLACE PACKAGE BODY my_pkg IS
```

```
    PRAGMA SERIALLY_REUSABLE;
    PROCEDURE gig_em IS
    ...
END my_pkg;
```

Package Initialization

The first time a user references a package element, the entire package is loaded into the SGA of the database instance to which the user is connected. That code is then shared by all sessions that have EXECUTE authority on the package.

Any package data is then instantiated into the session's User Global Area (UGA), a private area in either the SGA or the Process Global Area (PGA). If the package body contains an initialization section, that code will be executed. The initialization section is optional and appears at the end of the package body, beginning with a BEGIN statement and ending with the EXCEPTION section (if present) or the END of the package.

The following package initialization section runs a query to transfer the user's minimum balance into a global package variable. Programs can then reference the packaged variable (via the function) to retrieve the balance, rather than execute the query repeatedly:

```
CREATE OR REPLACE PACKAGE usrinfo
IS
    FUNCTION minbal RETURN VARCHAR2;
END usrinfo;

CREATE OR REPLACE PACKAGE BODY usrinfo
IS
    g_minbal NUMBER; -- Package-level data
    FUNCTION minbal RETURN VARCHAR2
    IS
    BEGIN
        RETURN g_minbal;
    END;
BEGIN  -- Initialization section
    SELECT minimum_balance
```

```
      INTO g_minbal
      FROM user_configuration
    WHERE username = USER;
EXCEPTION
   WHEN NO_DATA_FOUND
   THEN g_minbal := NULL;
END usrinfo;
```

Calling PL/SQL Functions in SQL

Stored functions can be called from SQL statements in a manner similar to built-in functions, such as DECODE, NVL, or RTRIM. This is a powerful technique for incorporating business rules into SQL in a simple and elegant way, but there are several caveats and restrictions.

The most notable caveat is that stored functions executed from SQL are not by default guaranteed to return results from the database that are read-consistent with respect to the parent SQL statement. Unless the SQL statement and any stored functions in that statement are in the same read-consistent transaction (even if they are read-only), each execution of the stored function may look at a different time-consistent set of data. To avoid this potential problem, you have two choices:

1. Restrict the stored function to perform only computations that do not involve using data from database tables.
2. Ensure read consistency programmatically by issuing the SET TRANSACTION READ ONLY or SET TRANSACTION ISOLATION LEVEL SERIALIZABLE statement before executing your SQL statement containing the stored function. A COMMIT or ROLLBACK then needs to follow the SQL statement to end this read-consistent transaction.

Calling a Function

The syntax for calling a stored function from SQL is the same as that used to reference it from PL/SQL:

```
[schema_name.][pkg_name.]func_name[@db_link]
[parm_list]
```

schema_name is optional and refers to the user/owner of the function or package. *pkg_name* is optional and refers to the package containing the called function. *func_name* is required and is the function name. *db_link* is optional and refers to the database link name to the remote database containing the function. *parm_list* is optional, as are the parameters passed to the function.

The following are example calls to the GetTimestamp function in the time_pkg example seen earlier in "Package Structure" on page 129:

```
-- Capture system events.
INSERT INTO v_sys_event
  (timestamp, event, qty_waits)
    SELECT time_pkg.GetTimestamp, event, total_waits
    FROM v$system_event

-- Capture system statistics.
INSERT INTO v_sys_stat (timestamp, stat#, value)
    SELECT time_pkg.GetTimestamp, statistic#, value
    FROM v$sysstat;
```

There are several requirements for calling stored functions in SQL:

- All parameters must be IN; no IN OUT or OUT parameters are allowed.

- The datatypes of the function's parameters and RETURN must be compatible with RDBMS datatypes. You cannot have arguments or RETURN types, such as BOOLEAN, programmer-defined record, and associative array.

- The function must be a schema-level object in the database or defined in the specification of a package.

Improving Performance of Calling PL/SQL Functions from SQL

Oracle Database 12c introduced the UDF pragma, which signals to the compiler that you would like your subprogram to be optimized for invocation from SQL statements. The GetTimestamp function mentioned previously would become:

```
...
    FUNCTION GetTimestamp RETURN DATE IS
        PRAGMA UDF;
    BEGIN
        RETURN StartTimeStamp;
    END GetTimestamp;
...
```

After compiling with this pragma, Oracle's runtime engine may be able to reduce the overhead associated with context switching, resulting in better performance. However, performance when called from inside PL/SQL is likely to be worse.

Another feature added in Oracle Database 12c is the ability to declare a function inside the WITH clause of a SELECT statement. If the UDF pragma is not helpful, you could explore this feature as a possible performance optimization. An example:

```
WITH
    FUNCTION betwnstr (str IN VARCHAR2,
      p1 IN INTEGER, p2 IN INTEGER)
    RETURN VARCHAR2
    IS
    BEGIN
        RETURN SUBSTR(str, p1, p2 - p1 +1);
    END;
SELECT betwnstr(last_name, 3, 5)
  FROM employees;
```

Column Name Versus Function Name Precedence

If your function has the same name as a table column in your SELECT statement, and the function has no parameter, the column takes precedence over the function. To force the Oracle database to resolve the name to your function, prepend the schema name to it:

```
CREATE TABLE emp(new_sal NUMBER ...);
CREATE FUNCTION new_sal RETURN NUMBER IS ...;

-- Resolves to column
SELECT new_sal FROM emp;
-- Resolves to function
SELECT scott.new_sal FROM emp;
```

Object-Oriented Features

In the Oracle database, an *object type* combines attributes (data structures) and methods (functions and procedures) into a single programming construct. The object type construct allows programmers to define their own reusable datatypes for use in PL/SQL programs and table and column definitions. An object type must be created in a database before it can be used in a PL/SQL program.

An instance of an object type is an *object* in the same way that a variable is an instance of a scalar type. As with scalars, objects are either *persistent* (stored in the database) or *transient* (stored only in PL/SQL variables). Objects can be stored in a database as a row in a table (a row object) or as a column in a table. A table of row objects can be created with syntax such as this:

```
CREATE TABLE table_name OF object_type;
```

When stored in such a table, the object (row) has a system-generated object identifier (OID) that is unique throughout the database.

Object Types

An object type has two parts: a specification and a body. The specification is required and contains the attributes and method specifications. The syntax for creating the object type specification is:

```
CREATE [OR REPLACE] TYPE obj_type_name
  [AUTHID { CURRENT_USER | DEFINER } ]
  [ACCESSIBLE BY (program_unit_list)]
{ { IS | AS } OBJECT | UNDER parent_type_name }
(
  attribute_name datatype,...,
  [ [ [NOT] OVERRIDING ] [ [NOT] FINAL ] [ [NOT]
    INSTANTIABLE ]
      method_spec,...,
  ]
)
[ [NOT] FINAL ]
[ [NOT] INSTANTIABLE ];
```

where *method_spec* is one of the following:

```
MEMBER { PROCEDURE | FUNCTION } program_spec
```

or:

```
STATIC { PROCEDURE | FUNCTION } program_spec
```

or:

```
{ ORDER | MAP } MEMBER FUNCTION comparison_func
tion_spec
```

or:

```
[ FINAL ] [ INSTANTIABLE ] CONSTRUCTOR FUNCTION
  RETURNING SELF AS RESULT constructor_func
tion_spec
```

Attribute specifications must appear before method specifications. Object attributes, like table columns, are defined with a name and a datatype. The name can be any legal identifier, and the datatype can be almost any datatype known to SQL other than LONG, LONG RAW, ROWID, and UROWID. Attributes can be declared using other programmer-defined object types or collection types, but not of the special types ANYTYPE, ANYDATA, or ANYDATASET. Attributes cannot be of datatypes unique to PL/SQL, such as BOOLEAN.

Method headers appear in the object type specification in a comma-delimited list. Unlike in a package specification, commas (not semicolons) terminate the object type program specifications. To support object comparisons and sorting, the type optionally can include one comparison method—either ORDER or MAP. Member methods can be overloaded in object types following the same rules as function and procedure overloading in packages.

Method "specs" that appear earlier in the syntax actually can be call specs for Java classes in the database or for external procedures written in C.

The syntax for creating the object type body is:

```
CREATE [OR REPLACE] TYPE BODY obj_type_name
{ IS | AS }
   method_implementation;
   [ method_implementation ... ]
;
```

Where method_implementation is one of:

```
MEMBER { PROCEDURE | FUNCTION } function_body
```

or:

```
STATIC { PROCEDURE | FUNCTION } function_body
```

or:

```
{ ORDER | MAP } MEMBER FUNCTION
                    comparison_function_body
```

or:

```
[ FINAL ] [ INSTANTIABLE ] CONSTRUCTOR FUNCTION
   RETURNING SELF AS RESULT
                    constructor_function_body
```

Again, the program bodies can be call specs to Java or C programs.

Type Inheritance

You can define subtypes of object types following a single-inheritance model. The database does not have a master root-level object; instead, each type is "standalone" unless declared otherwise.

The UNDER keyword specifies that the type exists as a subtype in a hierarchy. When you are using UNDER, the parent type must be marked NOT FINAL. By default, types are FINAL, meaning that you cannot declare a subtype of that type.

A subtype contains all the attributes and methods of its parent (supertype) and may contain additional attributes and methods. Methods can override corresponding methods from the parent. Changes to the supertype—such as the addition of attributes or methods—are reflected in the subtypes automatically.

By default, object types are INSTANTIABLE—that is, an invoking program may create an object of that type. The phrase NOT INSTANTIABLE indicates that you don't want any objects of the type, in which case the database will not create a constructor for it. This variation generally makes sense only with types that will serve as parents of other types.

Methods

There are four kinds of methods: *member*, *static*, *constructor*, and *comparison*.

Member methods

A member method is a procedure or function designated with the keyword MEMBER. Calling programs may invoke such a method only on objects that have been instantiated.

Static methods

A static method has no access to a current (SELF) object. Such a method is declared using the keyword STATIC and can be invoked at any time using *type.method* syntax.

Constructor methods

Even if you don't declare any methods, every instantiable object has a default constructor method that allows a calling program to create new objects of that type. This built-in method:

- Has the same name as the object type.

- Is a function that returns an object of that type.

- Accepts attributes in named or positional notation.

- Must be called with a value (or NULL) for every attribute —there is no DEFAULT clause for object attributes.

- Cannot be modified.

You can replace this default constructor with your own using the CONSTRUCTOR FUNCTION syntax. This method must have the same name as the object type, but there are no restrictions on its parameter list. The RETURN clause of the constructor's header must be RETURN SELF AS RESULT. The database supports overloading of programmer-defined constructors. All nonstatic methods have the implied parameter SELF, which refers to the current instance of the object. The default mode for the SELF parameter is IN for functions and IN OUT for procedures. A programmer can alter the mode by explicitly including SELF in the formal parameter list. An example of a programmer-defined default constructor follows:

```
CREATE OR REPLACE TYPE book_t AS OBJECT (
    isbn VARCHAR2(13),
    pages INTEGER,

    CONSTRUCTOR FUNCTION book_t
        (id IN INTEGER DEFAULT NULL
```

```
        ,title IN VARCHAR2 DEFAULT NULL
        ,isbn IN VARCHAR2 DEFAULT NULL
        ,pages IN INTEGER DEFAULT NULL
        )
    RETURN SELF AS RESULT,

    OVERRIDING MEMBER FUNCTION ck_digit_okay
        RETURN BOOLEAN,

    OVERRIDING MEMBER FUNCTION print
        RETURN VARCHAR2
    );
```

Comparison methods

The comparison methods, ORDER and MAP, establish ordinal positions of objects for comparisons such as "<" or "between" and for sorting (ORDER BY, GROUP BY, DISTINCT). The database invokes a comparison method automatically whenever it needs to perform such an operation.

MAP and ORDER methods are actually special types of member methods—that is, they execute only in the context of an existing object. An ORDER function accepts two parameters: SELF and another object of the same type. It must return an INTEGER value as explained in the following table:

Return value	Object comparison
Any negative integer (commonly −1)	SELF < second object
0	SELF = second object
Any positive integer (commonly 1)	SELF > second object
NULL	Undefined comparison: attributes needed for the comparison are NULL

For example, the Senate ranks majority party members higher than nonmajority party members and within the majority (or nonmajority) by years of service. Here is an example ORDER function incorporating these rules:

```
CREATE TYPE senator_t AS OBJECT
(
   majority INTEGER,
   yrs_service NUMBER,

   ORDER MEMBER FUNCTION ranking (
     other IN senator_t)
     RETURN INTEGER
 );

CREATE OR REPLACE TYPE BODY senator_t
AS
   ORDER MEMBER FUNCTION ranking (
     other IN senator_t)
     RETURN INTEGER
   IS
   BEGIN
      IF SELF.majority = 'Y' AND
         other.majority.istrue = 'Y'
      THEN
         RETURN SIGN(
           SELF.yrs_service -
           other.yrs_service);
      ELSIF SELF.majority = 'Y' AND
         other.majority ='N'
      THEN
         RETURN 1;
      ELSIF SELF.majority = 'N' AND
         other.majority.istrue = 'Y'
      THEN
         RETURN -1;
      ELSIF SELF.majority = 'N' AND
         other.majority.istrue = 'N'
      THEN
         RETURN SIGN(
           SELF.yrs_service -
           other.yrs_service);
      END IF;
```

```
    END ranking;
END;
```

A MAP function accepts no parameters and returns a scalar datatype such as DATE, NUMBER, or VARCHAR2 for which the database already knows a collating sequence. The MAP function translates, or *maps*, each object into this scalar datatype space.

If no ORDER or MAP function exists for an object type, then SQL, but not PL/SQL, supports only limited equality comparisons of objects. Objects are equal if they are of the same object type and if each attribute is equal.

Use MAP if possible when frequently sorting or comparing a large number of objects, as in a SQL statement; an internal optimization reduces the number of function calls. With ORDER, the function must run once for every comparison.

Methods in Subtypes

When defining methods in a subtype, you have two options: you can *inherit* a supertype's method, or you can *override* a supertype's method by defining your own subtype method of the same name and parameter list. If you choose to inherit, you do not need to write any code in the subtype.

To override a supertype, you must use the OVERRIDING keyword in the header of the program, as shown here:

```
CREATE TYPE food_t AS OBJECT (
    name VARCHAR2(100),
    food_group  VARCHAR2 (100),
    MEMBER FUNCTION price RETURN NUMBER
    )
NOT FINAL;

CREATE TYPE dessert_t UNDER food_t (
    contains_chocolate CHAR(1),
    OVERRIDING MEMBER FUNCTION price RETURN NUMBER
    );
```

This example also shows that if you want to allow a method to be overridden, you must specify that this method be NOT FINAL. By default, methods are FINAL and cannot be overridden.

You also can define a method to be NOT INSTANTIABLE, which means that you specify only the header of the method, but you do not need to provide an implementation in the OBJECT TYPE body for that method. For example:

```
CREATE TYPE food_t AS OBJECT (
    name VARCHAR2(100),
    food_group  VARCHAR2 (100),
    NOT INSTANTIABLE MEMBER
      FUNCTION price RETURN NUMBER
    )
NOT FINAL
NOT INSTANTIABLE;
```

The consequences of a NOT INSTANTIABLE method are as follows:

- The entire object type must be defined as NOT INSTANTIABLE, which means that you cannot instantiate an instance from this type. You can use it only as a supertype in an object type hierarchy.

- Any subtype of food_t must provide an implementation of the price function or in turn also be defined as a NOT INSTANTIABLE object type.

The database supports *dynamic method dispatch*, also known as *dynamic polymorphism*, to determine which overridden method to invoke at runtime. That is, it will choose the method in the most specific subtype associated with the currently instantiated object. However, it is also possible to directly invoke a parent type's method. For example, you can invoke the food_t version of a dessert's price method using the following syntax:

```
DECLARE
   my_dessert dessert_t := dessert_t (
      'tres leches', 'sugar', 'N');
BEGIN
   DBMS_OUTPUT.PUT_LINE(
         (my_dessert AS food_t).price);
END;
```

This is also possible inside the implementation sections of sub-type methods using SELF:

```
(SELF AS parent_type).method_invocation;
```

Manipulating Objects in PL/SQL and SQL

Variables declared as objects begin their life *atomically null*, meaning that the expression:

```
object IS NULL
```

evaluates to TRUE. Attempting to assign values to the attributes of an atomically null object will return an ACCESS_INTO_NULL exception. Instead, you must initialize the object, in one of these ways:

- Use either the default constructor method or a user-defined constructor
- Assign to it the value of an existing object
- Use SELECT INTO or FETCH INTO

Here is an example using each initialization technique:

```
DECLARE
   project_boiler_plate    project_t;
   build_web_site          project_t;

   -- Initialize via constructor.
   new_web_mgr  proj_mgr_t :=
      proj_mgr_t('Ruth', 'Home Office');

   -- Initialize via user-defined constructor
```

```
   -- that provides defaults
   new_web_mgr proj_mgr_t := NEW proj_mgr_t();

   CURSOR template_cur IS
      SELECT VALUE(proj)
        FROM projects
       WHERE project_type = 'TEMPLATE'
             AND sub_type = 'WEB SITE';
BEGIN
   OPEN template_cur;
   -- Initialize via FETCH INTO.
   FETCH template_cur INTO project_boiler_plate;

   -- Initialize via assignment.
   build_web_site := project_boiler_plate;
   ...
```

After an object is initialized, it can be stored in the database, and you can then locate and use that object with the REF, VALUE, and DEREF operators.

Upcasting and Downcasting

The Oracle database supports implicit *upcasting* (widening) of a subtype and provides the TREAT operator to *downcast* (narrow) a supertype. TREAT also can explicitly upcast a subtype.

The following example returns to the food-dessert hierarchy to demonstrate upcasting and downcasting:

```
CREATE TYPE food_t AS OBJECT (
   name VARCHAR2(100),
   food_group  VARCHAR2 (100)
)
NOT FINAL;

CREATE TYPE dessert_t UNDER food_t (
   contains_chocolate CHAR(1)
);

DECLARE
```

```
marzipan dessert_t :=
  NEW dessert_t('marzipan', 'sweets', 'N');
ice_cream_sundae dessert_t;
tasty_treat food_t;
BEGIN
  /* An implied upcast */
  tasty_treat := marzipan;

  /* An explicit downcast */
  ice_cream_sundae :=
    TREAT(tasty_treat AS dessert_t);
END;
```

The syntax of TREAT is:

```
TREAT (object_instance AS [REF] type)
```

where *object_instance* is a value that is of a particular supertype in an object hierarchy, and *type* is the name of the subtype (or supertype) in the same hierarchy. The TREAT expression won't compile if you attempt to cast a type to another from a different type hierarchy. If you supply an object from the correct type hierarchy, TREAT will return either the casted object or NULL —but not an error.

You also can use dot notation to obtain access to the casted object's attributes and methods:

```
TREAT (object_instance AS type).{ attribute |
method(args...) } ]
```

SQL also supports TREAT and implied upcasting.

REF operator

REF, short for REFerence, designates a datatype modifier or an operator to retrieve a logical pointer to an object. This pointer encapsulates the OID and can simplify navigation among related database objects. The syntax for a REF operator is:

```
REF(table_alias_name)
```

For example:

```
SELECT REF(p) FROM pets p WHERE ...
```

A PL/SQL variable can hold a reference to a particular object type:

```
DECLARE
   petref REF Pet_t;
BEGIN
   SELECT REF(p) INTO petref FROM pets p WHERE ...
```

Through deletions, REFs can reference a nonexistent object, called a *dangling REF*, resulting in a state that can be detected with the IS DANGLING predicate. For example:

```
UPDATE pets
   SET owner_ref = NULL
 WHERE owner_ref IS DANGLING;
```

The built-in package UTL_REF provides programmatic access to stored objects via their REF.

VALUE operator

Use the VALUE operator to retrieve a row object as a single object rather than as multiple columns. The syntax for the VALUE operator is:

```
VALUE(table_alias_name)
```

For example:

```
SELECT VALUE(p) FROM pets p WHERE ...
```

DEREF operator

Use the DEREF operator to retrieve the value of an object for which you have a REF. The syntax for DEREF is:

```
DEREF(table_alias_name)
```

For example:

```
DECLARE
   person_ref    REF person_t;
   author        person_t;
```

```
BEGIN
   -- Get the ref.
   SELECT REF(p) INTO person_ref
      FROM persons WHERE p.last_name ='Pribyl';

   -- Dereference the pointer back to the value.
   SELECT DEREF(person_ref) INTO author FROM dual;
```

In addition, the database uses an OID internally as a unique identifier for each object. As with a ROWID, you don't typically use an OID directly. The following table shows ways of referencing persistent objects:

Scheme	Description	Applications
OID	An opaque, globally unique handle, produced when the object is stored in the database as a table (row) object.	The persistent object's handle; it is what REFs point to. Your program never uses it directly.
VALUE	An operator. In SQL, it acts on an object in an object table and returns the object's *contents*. Different from the VALUES keyword found in some INSERT statements.	Used when fetching a table (row) object into a variable, or when you need to refer to an object table as an object instead of a list of columns.
REF	A pointer to an object. May be used within a SQL statement as an operator or in a declaration as a type modifier.	Allows quasi-normalizing of object-relational databases and joining of object tables using dot navigation. In PL/SQL, REFs serve as input/output variables.
DEREF	Reverse pointer lookup for REFs.	Used for retrieving the contents of an object when all you know is its REF.

Changing Object Types

You can add methods, but not attributes, to an object type stored in the database using the ALTER TYPE statement. There are several forms of this statement, with many options, some of which are in the following code block. Check Oracle documentation for the most up-to-date syntax diagrams:

```
ALTER TYPE typename
    { ADD | MODIFY | DROP } ATTRIBUTE attribute_spec
    { INVALIDATE | CASCADE
    { [ NOT ] INCLUDING TABLE DATA |
        CONVERT TO SUBSTITUTABLE }
    [ FORCE ] };

ALTER TYPE typename
    [ NOT ] { INSTANTIABLE | FINAL }
    { INVALIDATE | CASCADE
        { [ NOT ] INCLUDING TABLE DATA |
            CONVERT TO SUBSTITUTABLE }
        [ FORCE ] };

ALTER TYPE typename
    COMPILE [ DEBUG ] [ SPECIFICATION | BODY ]
    [ REUSE SETTINGS ];
```

Because altering the structure of a type can have quite a few repercussions for database objects, the database requires that you either INVALIDATE the dependent objects or CASCADE the change.

When making a change from FINAL to NOT FINAL and cascading the change, you can cause existing table objects to be either NOT SUBSTITUTABLE (the default) or SUBSTITUTABLE. The following is an example of adding an attribute:

```
ALTER TYPE catalog_item_t
    ADD ATTRIBUTE publication_date VARCHAR2(400)
    CASCADE INCLUDING TABLE DATA;
```

The next example shows adding a method:

```
ALTER TYPE catalog_item_t
    ADD MEMBER PROCEDURE save,
    CASCADE;
```

After adding a method to a spec, you would use CREATE OR REPLACE TYPE BODY to implement it in the body (include all the other methods as well).

There are a variety of restrictions on modifying types; for example, you cannot change a type from INSTANTIABLE to NOT INSTANTIABLE if you have created tables that depend on the type.

The syntax for dropping an object type is:

```
DROP TYPE typename [FORCE];
```

You can drop only an object type that has not been implemented in a table (or you can drop the tables first). The FORCE option will drop object types even if they have dependencies, but FORCE will irreversibly invalidate any dependent objects such as tables. FORCE does not do a DROP CASCADE.

If you are dropping a type whose parent type has table dependents, this form of the statement:

```
DROP TYPE subtype_name VALIDATE;
```

will "validate" the safety of dropping the subtype before performing it. That is, the database will perform the drop only if there are no objects of the subtype in any substitutable columns of the parent type.

Compilation

PL/SQL compilation is an area that has seen several improvements in recent database versions. These capabilities include conditional compilation, informational warnings, optimization, and compilation to native code.

Compiling Stored PL/SQL Programs

The following keywords are available when creating stored programs:

OR REPLACE
> Used with CREATE to rebuild an existing program unit, preserving privileges granted on it to users and roles.

AUTHID
> Defines whether the program will execute with the privileges of, and resolve names like, the object owner (DEFINER), or as the user executing the function (CURRENT_USER). The default AUTHID is DEFINER. See "Privileges and Stored PL/SQL" on page 118 for additional information.

ACCESSIBLE BY (program unit list)
> (Oracle Database 12*c* and later.) Restricts execution of the program to a white list of other programs. Useful when you want to hide some utility programs behind your stable API.

DETERMINISTIC
> Required for function-based indexes. A function is DETERMINISTIC if it always returns the same value when called with the same parameters. Deterministic functions do not meaningfully reference package variables or the database. The built-in INITCAP is deterministic, but SYSDATE is not.

PARALLEL_ENABLE...
> Informs the optimizer that a function is safe for parallel execution. Can improve runtime performance of pipelined table functions that are called in a parallel SQL query.

PIPELINED
> Used with table functions. Specifies that the results of this table function should be returned iteratively via the PIPE ROW statement. A pipelined function can start to return data as it is generated instead of all at once after processing is complete.

AGGREGATE USING

Required for aggregate functions. Tells the database that the function evaluates a group of rows and returns a single result. For example, the built-in function AVG is an aggregate function.

The following compiler settings are established at program creation time based on the database or session configuration and can be changed or retained during recompilation. The database stores these compiler settings on a program-by-program basis, so you can recompile your program later using the REUSE SETTINGS option. If you do not reuse the stored settings, or if you explicitly define one or more settings, your current session settings are used:

PLSQL_CCFLAGS

Contains a comma-delimited list of name:value pairs controlling conditional compilation. See "Conditional Compilation" on page 155 for more information.

PLSQL_CODE_TYPE

Controls whether interpreted or native code is created during compilation. Valid values are INTERPRETED or NATIVE. See "Performing Native Compilation of PL/SQL" on page 163 for more information.

PLSQL_DEBUG

Controls whether or not the program will be instrumented for debugging during compilation. Valid values are TRUE or FALSE. When compiled for debugging, a program will always be INTERPRETED and never NATIVE.

PLSQL_OPTIMIZE_LEVEL

Controls the level of optimization employed by the compiler. Valid values are 0, 1, 2, or 3. See "Optimizing Compiler" on page 161 for more information.

PLSQL_WARNINGS
> Controls the level of warnings that the compiler will report. See "Compiler Warnings" on page 158 for more information.

NLS_LENGTH_SEMANTICS
> Controls whether VARCHAR2 and CHAR datatypes are defined with BYTE (default) or CHAR semantics. NVARCHAR2, NCHAR, CLOB, and NCLOB datatypes are always defined with CHAR semantics.

To recompile the procedure my_proc, explicitly setting the optimization level to 3, run the following:

```
ALTER PROCEDURE my_proc COMPILE PLSQL_OPTIMIZE_
LEVEL = 3;
```

Then to recompile it later with the saved settings, run the following:

```
ALTER PROCEDURE my_proc COMPILE REUSE SETTINGS;
```

To view all of the stored compiler settings for your programs, query the view USER_PLSQL_OBJECT_SETTINGS.

Conditional Compilation

Conditional compilation allows your programs to decide at compile time which blocks of code will be implemented. You can conditionally include code in the compiled program based on the database version, environment, or other configurable settings. There are three types of compiler directives available for you to use:

Selection directives
> Use the $IF directive to evaluate an expression and determine which code should be included. For example:

```
DECLARE
   emp_rec employees%ROWTYPE;
BEGIN
$IF DBMS_DB_VERSION.VER_LE_10_2 $THEN
   -- Legacy code
   SELECT employees_seq.NEXTVAL
   INTO emp_rec.employee_id FROM dual;
$ELSE
   -- Oracle Database 11g and higher
   emp_rec.employee_id := employees_seq.NEXTVAL;
$END
   INSERT INTO emp VALUES (emp_rec);
END;
```

Inquiry directives

Use the $$identifier directive to refer to conditional compilation flags (PLSQL_CCFLAGS). These inquiry directives can be referenced in an $IF directive or independently. For example:

```
ALTER SESSION SET PLSQL_CCFLAGS =
   'pl_debug:false, pl_trace_level:2';

CREATE OR REPLACE PROCEDURE extract_client_data
AS
BEGIN
$IF $$pl_debug OR $$pl_trace_level >= 2 $THEN
   DBMS_SUPPORT.START_TRACE
      (waits=>TRUE, binds=>TRUE);
$ELSIF $$pl_trace_level >= 1 $THEN
   DBMS_SUPPORT.START_TRACE
      (waits=>TRUE, binds=>FALSE);
$END
   NULL; -- code goes here
END extract_client_data;
```

Error directives

Use the $ERROR directive to force compilation errors if your prerequisite conditions are not met. For example, I want to *make sure* no one compiles a compute-intensive program with a level below 2:

Check Out Receipt

Saskatoon - J.S. Wood Branch
306-975-7590
http://www.saskatoonlibrary.ca

Tuesday, May 22, 2018 5:58:00 PM
34715

Item: 39085901405296
Title: Oracle PL/SQL language pocket
reference
Material: Book
Due: 06/12/2018

Total items: 1

You just saved $22.71 by using your
library. You have saved $73.50 so far
this year by using your library!

Thank you! If you would like to update
your library notification to telephone,
email or text message, please contact
your local library.

```
CREATE OR REPLACE PROCEDURE compute_intensive IS
BEGIN
$IF $$plsql_optimize_level < 2
$THEN
   $ERROR 'Must use full optimization!' $END
$END
   NULL;
END;
```

The settings that are available for use in these directives include:

Compiler settings
> PLSCOPE_SETTINGS, PLSQL_CCFLAGS,
> PLSQL_DEBUG, PLSQL_WARNINGS, PLSQL_OPTI-
> MIZE_LEVEL, PLSQL_CODE_TYPE, and
> NLS_LENGTH_SEMANTICS.

PLSQL_LINE (PLS_INTEGER literal)
> The line number within the program or can be explicitly
> defined with the PLSQL_CCFLAGS parameter.

PLSQL_UNIT (VARCHAR2 literal)
> The name of the program being compiled. For anonymous
> blocks, it is null. PLSQL_UNIT can also be explicitly
> defined with the PLSQL_CCFLAGS parameter.

Static expressions defined in package specifications
> These expressions cannot change when a package is
> recompiled.

The PL/SQL compiler reads and interprets these directives, generating the code to be implemented. To identify what has actually been deployed in the compiled program, use the DBMS_PREPROCESSOR package, as in the following example:

```
-- Compile with conditional compilation statements
CREATE OR REPLACE PROCEDURE my_cc_proc IS
BEGIN
   DBMS_OUTPUT.PUT_LINE('DB Version is:'
      ||DBMS_DB_VERSION.VERSION||'r'
```

```
        ||DBMS_DB_VERSION.RELEASE);
$IF DBMS_DB_VERSION.VER_LE_11 $THEN
    DBMS_OUTPUT.PUT_LINE('Version 11 code here');
$ELSIF DBMS_DB_VERSION.VER_LE_12 $THEN
    DBMS_OUTPUT.PUT_LINE('Version 12 code here');
$END
END;
/

-- Display the deployed code
BEGIN
    DBMS_PREPROCESSOR.PRINT_POST_PROCESSED_SOURCE
        ('PROCEDURE', USER, 'MY_CC_PROC');
END;
```

This displays the following text (note that whitespace is preserved--and intentionally displayed here to ensure line numbers at runtime correspond to original source code):

```
PROCEDURE my_cc_proc IS
BEGIN
    DBMS_OUTPUT.PUT_LINE('DB Version is:'
        ||DBMS_DB_VERSION.VERSION||'r'
        ||DBMS_DB_VERSION.RELEASE);
    DBMS_OUTPUT.PUT_LINE('Version 12 code here');

END;
```

Compiler Warnings

Compile-time warnings can help make your programs more robust. These warnings highlight potential problems that are not severe enough to raise an exception, but may result in runtime errors or poor performance. You can configure the compiler to reject as an error any of these warnings. Warnings result in the program compiling to a VALID status, but errors result in an INVALID status.

To enable these warnings, you need to set the database initialization parameter PLSQL_WARNINGS. This parameter can be set globally in the *SPFILE* initialization file, in your session via

---

the ALTER SESSION statement, or with the built-in package DBMS_WARNING.

The PLSQL_WARNINGS parameter is a comma-delimited list of values, each of which has the syntax:

```
[ENABLE | DISABLE | ERROR] : [ALL | SEVERE |
INFORMATIONAL
| PERFORMANCE | warning_number]
```

For example, to enable all warnings in your session, execute:

```
ALTER SESSION SET plsql_warnings = 'enable:all';
```

If you want to configure warning message number 06009 ("OTHERS handler does not end in RAISE or RAISE_APPLI-CATION_ERROR") as an error and enable all warnings in the performance category except warning number 07202 ("Parameter may benefit from use of the NOCOPY compiler hint"), execute:

```
ALTER SESSION SET plsql_warnings =
    'error:06009'
  ,'enable:performance'
  ,'disable:07203';
```

To see what your current setting is, you can execute:

```
DBMS_OUTPUT.PUT_LINE
  (DBMS_WARNING.get_warning_setting_string());
```

Some examples of warnings follow (edited for space reasons):

```
SQL>ALTER SESSION SET plsql_warnings ='ENABLE:ALL';
Session altered.

SQL>CREATE OR REPLACE PROCEDURE bad_practice IS
  2    test_string VARCHAR2(32);
  3  BEGIN
  4    test_string := 'My demo program';
  5  EXCEPTION
  6    WHEN OTHERS THEN NULL;
  7  END;
  8  /
```

Warning: Procedure created with compilation errors.

```
SQL>SHOW ERRORS
    LINE/COL ERROR
    ---- -------------------------------------------
    4/1    PLW-07206: analysis suggests that the
           assignment to 'TEST_STRING' may be
           unnecessary

    6/6    PLS-06009: procedure "BAD_PRACTICE"
           OTHERS handler does not
           end in RAISE or RAISE_APPLICATION_ERROR

SQL> CREATE OR REPLACE PACKAGE create_policy IS
2 PROCEDURE proc_dec_page (dec_page IN OUT CLOB);
3 END create_policy;
4
/

SP2-0808: Package created with compilation warnings

SQL> SHOW ERRORS
Errors for PACKAGE CREATE_POLICY:

LINE/COL ERROR
---- -------------------------------------------
2/32   PLW-07203: parameter 'DEC_PAGE' may benefit
       from use of the NOCOPY compiler hint

SQL> CREATE OR REPLACE PACKAGE BODY create_policy
IS
2 PROCEDURE process_dec_page (
3 dec_page IN OUT NOCOPY CLOB ) IS
4 BEGIN
5 default_dec(dec_page);
6 END process_dec_page;
7 END create_policy;
8 /
SP2-0810: Package Body created with compilation
warnings
```

```
SQL> SHOW ERRORS
Errors for PACKAGE BODY CREATE_POLICY:

LINE/COL ERROR
---   ---------------------------------------------
3/6   PLW-05000: mismatch in NOCOPY qualification
      between specification and body

SQL> CREATE OR REPLACE PROCEDURE dead_code IS
2 x NUMBER := 10;
3 BEGIN
4 IF x = 10 THEN
5 x := 20;
6 ELSE
7 x := 100; -- dead code
8 END IF;
9 END dead_code;
10 /
SP2-0804: Procedure created with compilation
warnings

SQL> SHOW ERRORS
Errors for PROCEDURE DEAD_CODE:

LINE/COL ERROR
----  ----------------------------------------
7/7   PLW-06002: Unreachable code
```

Optimizing Compiler

PL/SQL's optimizing compiler can improve runtime performance dramatically while imposing only a relatively slight overhead at compile time. Fortunately, the benefits of optimization apply to both interpreted and natively compiled PL/SQL because optimizations are applied by analyzing patterns in source code.

The optimizing compiler is enabled by default. However, you may want to alter its behavior, by either lowering its aggressiveness or disabling it entirely. For example, if, in the course of normal operations, your system must perform recompilation of many lines of code, or if an application generates many lines of dynamically executed PL/SQL, the overhead of optimization may be unacceptable. Note, however, that Oracle's tests show that the optimizer doubles the runtime performance of computationally intensive PL/SQL.

In some cases, the optimizer may even alter program behavior. One such case might occur in code written for Oracle9i Database, which depends on the relative timing of initialization sections in multiple packages. If your testing demonstrates such a problem, yet you want to enjoy the performance benefits of the optimizer, you may want to rewrite the offending code or introduce an initialization routine that ensures the desired order of execution.

The Orace database utilizes *intra-unit inline optimization*. This optimization technique replaces a call to a subprogram with a copy of the program, at compile time. The performance improvement occurs because the subprogram does not have to be loaded separately at runtime. This technique is especially useful for short utility helper programs.

To change the optimizer settings, set the initialization parameter PLSQL_OPTIMIZE_LEVEL, either for your session with an ALTER SESSION statement or for the database with an ALTER SYSTEM statement. Valid settings are:

0

No optimization

1

Moderate optimization, such as eliminating superfluous code or exceptions

2 (default)

Aggressive optimization beyond level 1, including rearranging source code

---

3
Include inline subprogram optimization

You can also modify these settings for the current session; for example:

```
ALTER SESSION SET PLSQL_OPTIMIZE_LEVEL = 0;
```

With optimization level 2, you can control inline optimization with the INLINE pragma (see "Pragmas" on page 9). The syntax of the INLINE pragma is:

```
PRAGMA INLINE (program_name,'YES | NO');
```

YES requests the compiler to use inline optimization for calls to *program_name*, while NO explicitly requests the compiler to not use inline optimization for such calls. In the following example, compiled with the default optimization level 2, calls to the procedure P are requested to be inlined:

```
CREATE OR REPLACE PACKAGE BODY bi_util IS
  FUNCTION avg_sales(cust_id IN NUMBER)
    RETURN NUMBER
  IS
  BEGIN
  -- inline calls to program P
    PRAGMA INLINE (P,'YES');
    p('Inside simulation');
    RETURN cust_id; -- simulation only
  END;
END bi_util;
```

Performing Native Compilation of PL/SQL

You can speed up many of your PL/SQL programs by compiling them into code native to the hardware rather than using the default, system-independent compiled form (known as DIANA). Using native compilation, you will realize the greatest performance gains with computer-intensive applications and the least from programs that contain only declarations, such as types and package specifications. Note, though, that if you are working in development mode and need to compile a program with debug information, the native compilation feature is not available. Follow these steps to compile a stored program natively:

```
ALTER SESSION SET PLSQL_CODE_TYPE = 'NATIVE';
```

1. Ensure that database (or session-level) parameter PLSQL_OPTIMIZE_LEVEL is set to 2 or higher.

2. Set the database parameter PLSQL_CODE_TYPE to NATIVE, or issue a session-level statement:

3. Recompile your stored program.

If you want to recompile all your stored programs natively, follow the step-by-step procedure in Oracle's PL/SQL documentation (search for "Compiling the Entire Database for PL/SQL Native or Interpreted Compilation").

Java Language Integration

Java programmers can write server-side classes that invoke SQL and PL/SQL using standard JDBC or SQLJ calls. PL/SQL programmers can call server-side Java methods by writing a PL/SQL cover or *call spec* for Java using Oracle database DDL.

Server-side Java in the database may be faster than PL/SQL for computer-intensive programs, but not as nimble for database access. PL/SQL is much more efficient for database-intensive routines because, unlike Java, it doesn't have to pay the overhead for converting SQL datatypes for use inside the stored program. In my experience, the most common use of Java stored procedures is to supplement functionality not provided by Oracle built-ins (for example, to obtain a sorted listing of a directory in the host filesystem).

Follow these steps to create a Java stored procedure (JSP):

1. Write or otherwise obtain functional Java code. Having source code is not necessary, though, so you can use class libraries from third parties. The classes must meet two

requirements: methods published to SQL and PL/SQL must be declared static, because PL/SQL has no mechanism for instantiating nonstatic Java classes; and, the classes must not issue any GUI calls (for example, to AWT) at runtime.

If you write your own JSP and it needs to connect to the database for access to tables or stored procedures, use standard JDBC and/or SQLJ calls in your code. Many JDBC and SQLJ reference materials are available to provide assistance in calling SQL or PL/SQL from Java, but be sure to review the product-specific documentation that ships with your tool.

2. Once you have the Java class in hand, either in source or *.class* file format, load it into the database. The database's loadjava command-line utility is a convenient way to accomplish the load. Refer to the *Oracle Java Developer's Guide* for further assistance with loadjava.

3. Create a call spec for the Java method, specifying the AS LANGUAGE JAVA clause of the CREATE statement (described in "Publishing Java to PL/SQL" on page 166). You may create a function or procedure cover as appropriate.

4. Grant EXECUTE privileges on the new JSP using GRANT EXECUTE; PL/SQL routines can now call the JSP as if it were another PL/SQL module.

Example

Let's write a simple "Hello, World" JSP that will accept an argument:

```
package oreilly.plsquick.demos;

public class Hello {
   public static String sayIt (String toWhom) {
      return "Hello, " + toWhom + "!";
   }
}
```

Saved in a file called *Hello.java*, the source code can be loaded directly into the database. Doing so will compile the code automatically. Here is a simple form of the *loadjava* command:

```
loadjava -user scott/tiger oreilly/plsquick/demos/
Hello.java
```

The *Hello.java* file follows the Java file placement convention for packages, and thus exists in a subdirectory named *oreilly/plsquick/demos*.

We can fire up our favorite SQL interpreter, connect as SCOTT/TIGER, and create the call spec for the Hello.sayIt() method:

```
CREATE FUNCTION hello_there (to_whom IN VARCHAR2)
   RETURN VARCHAR2
   AS LANGUAGE JAVA
   NAME 'oreilly.plsquick.demos.Hello.sayIt
     (java.lang.String) return java.lang.String';
```

Now we can call our function very easily:

```
BEGIN
   DBMS_OUTPUT.PUT_LINE(hello_there('world'));
END;
```

And we get the following as the expected output:

```
Hello, world!
```

Publishing Java to PL/SQL

To write a call spec, use the AS LANGUAGE JAVA clause in a CREATE statement. The syntax for this clause is:

```
{ IS | AS } LANGUAGE JAVA
   NAME 'method_fullname [ (type_fullname,... ]
     [ RETURN type_fullname ]'
```

method_fullname is the package-qualified name of the Java class and method. It is case-sensitive and uses dots to separate parts of the package's full name. *type_fullname* is the package-qualified name of the Java datatype. Notice that a literal string, not a SQL identifier, follows the NAME keyword.

Type mapping follows most JDBC rules regarding the legal mapping of SQL types to Java types. JDBC extensions exist for Oracle-specific datatypes. Most datatype mappings are relatively straightforward, but passing database objects of a user-defined type is harder than one would think. Oracle provides a tool named JPublisher that generates the Java required to encapsulate a database object and its corresponding REF. Refer to Oracle's JPublisher documentation for guidelines on usage.

The AS LANGUAGE JAVA clause is the same regardless of whether you are using Java as a standalone JSP, the implementation of a packaged program, or the body of an object type method. For example, here is the complete syntax for creating JSPs as PL/SQL-callable functions or procedures:

```
CREATE [OR REPLACE]
{ PROCEDURE procedure_name [(param[, param]...)]
  | FUNCTION function_name [(param[, param]...)]
     RETURN sql_type
}
[AUTHID {DEFINER | CURRENT_USER}]
[PARALLEL_ENABLE]
[DETERMINISTIC]
{ IS | AS } LANGUAGE JAVA
   NAME 'method_fullname [ (type_fullname,... ]
     [ RETURN type_fullname ]'
```

When using Java as the implementation of a packaged procedure or function, the database allows you to place the Java call spec either in the package specification (where the call spec substitutes for the subprogram specification) or in the package body (where the call spec substitutes for the subprogram body). Similarly, when using JSPs in object type methods, the Java call spec can substitute for either the object type method specification or its body.

Note that Java functions typically map to PL/SQL functions, but Java functions declared void map to PL/SQL procedures. Also, you will quickly learn that mistakes in mapping PL/SQL parameters to Java parameters become evident only at runtime.

Data Dictionary

To learn what Java library units are available in your schema, look in the USER_OBJECTS data dictionary view where the *object_type* is like "JAVA%". If you see a Java class with INVALID status, it has not yet been resolved successfully. Note that the names of the Java source library units need not match the names of the classes they produce.

Index

Get even more for your money.

Join the O'Reilly Community, and register the O'Reilly books you own. It's free, and you'll get:

- $4.99 ebook upgrade offer
- 40% upgrade offer on O'Reilly print books
- Membership discounts on books and events
- Free lifetime updates to ebooks and videos
- Multiple ebook formats, DRM FREE
- Participation in the O'Reilly community
- Newsletters
- Account management
- 100% Satisfaction Guarantee

Signing up is easy:

1. Go to: oreilly.com/go/register
2. Create an O'Reilly login.
3. Provide your address.
4. Register your books.

Note: English-language books only

To order books online:
oreilly.com/store

For questions about products or an order:
orders@oreilly.com

To sign up to get topic-specific email announcements and/or news about upcoming books, conferences, special offers, and new technologies:
elists@oreilly.com

For technical questions about book content:
booktech@oreilly.com

To submit new book proposals to our editors:
proposals@oreilly.com

O'Reilly books are available in multiple DRM-free ebook formats. For more information:
oreilly.com/ebooks

O'REILLY®

The information you need, when and where you need it.

With Safari Books Online, you can:

Access the contents of thousands of technology and business books

- Quickly search over 7000 books and certification guides
- Download whole books or chapters in PDF format, at no extra cost, to print or read on the go
- Copy and paste code
- Save up to 35% on O'Reilly print books
- **New!** Access mobile-friendly books directly from cell phones and mobile devices

Stay up-to-date on emerging topics before the books are published

- Get on-demand access to evolving manuscripts.
- Interact directly with authors of upcoming books

Explore thousands of hours of video on technology and design topics

- Learn from expert video tutorials
- Watch and replay recorded conference sessions

safaribooksonline.com

CPSIA information can be obtained at www.ICGtesting.com
Printed in the USA
BVOW06n2224130915

417685BV00006B/10/P

9 781491 920008